D0791981

ANIMAL BEHAVIOR

Animal Migration

CHRISTINA WILSDON

ANIMAL BEHAVIOR

Animal Communication
Animal Courtship
Animal Defenses
Animal Hunting and Feeding
Animal Life in Groups
Animal Migration

GRETEL H. SCHUELLER AND SHEILA K. SCHUELLER

Chelsea House
An imprint of Infobase Publishing
132 West 31st Street
New York NY 10001

Library of Congress Cataloging-in-Publication Data

Schueller, Gretel H.
Animal migration / Gretel H. Schueller and Sheila K. Schueller.
p. cm. — (Animal behavior)
Includes bibliographical references and index.
ISBN 978-1-60413-127-7 (hardcover)
1. Animal migration I. Schueller, Sheila K. II. Title. III. Series.

QL754.S37 2009
591.56'8—dc22 2008040125

Chelsea House books are available at special discounts when purchased in bulk quantities for businesses, associations, institutions, or sales promotions. Please call our Special Sales Department in New York at (212) 967-8800 or (800) 322-8755.

You can find Chelsea House on the World Wide Web at http://www.chelseahouse.com

Text design by Kerry Casey
Cover design by Ben Peterson
Printed in the United States
Bang EJB 10 9 8 7 6 5 4 3 2 1
This book is printed on acid-free paper.

All links and Web addresses were checked and verified to be correct at the time of publication. Because of the dynamic nature of the Web, some addresses and links may have changed since publication and may no longer be valid.

Cover: Barnacle geese take flight.

Contents

1

Discovering Migration: What Birds Reveal

A SNOW-COVERED FOREST in winter can be a quiet place. Come spring, however, this same spot will be filled with the chirps, chatter, and calls of birds. Where did they go during the winter?

Long ago, some people used to think that during the winter, birds slept in holes that they dug in the ground. Others thought they hid in the mud on the bottoms of ponds—alive, but waiting for spring. Others claimed that familiar summer birds transformed into other types of birds in the winter. The truth is, in some ways, more unbelievable. What birds do during this time is fly: They fly over land and oceans—without a roadmap or compass—to destinations that are sometimes thousands of miles away. Like marathon runners, birds pace themselves so they do not run out of energy before they can land. They are always adjusting speed, height, and flight path to account for changing winds, their own weight, and storms. In the spring, they retrace their paths back to their summer homes. They do this every year. In other words, they migrate.

Migration is the movement of animals from one location to another and back again. Migrations are usually seasonal and relate to an animal's need to feed or reproduce. For example, each

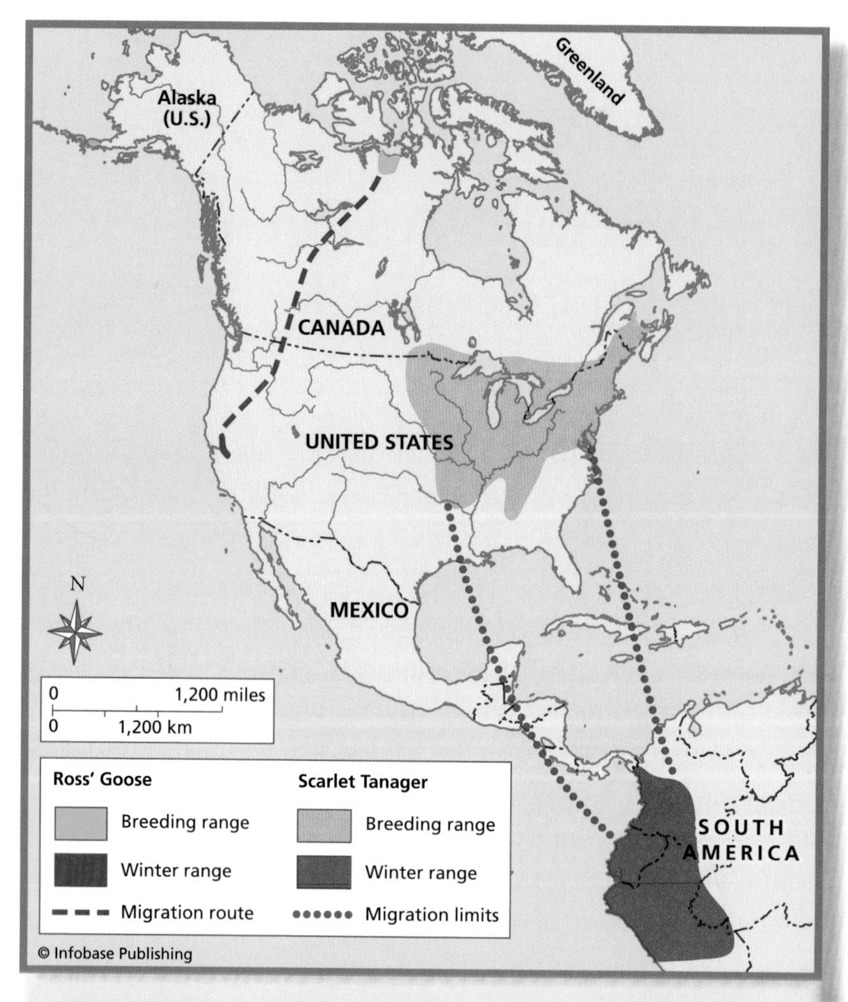

Different birds have different breeding locations and migrations paths. Ross's geese breed in the Arctic and then migrate south through Canada and to the United States. There, they turn southwest to winter in California, unlike other birds they fly with that turn southeast toward the Gulf Coast. Scarlet tanagers' migration range stretches from the United States to South America. After breeding in various parts of the United States, they fly south in the fall.

fall, about five billion birds migrate south for the winter from North America. Nearly all North American birds migrate: 500 of the 650 **species**. Yet this is just one small part of the picture. More than half of all the bird species in the world—approximately 5,000 species—migrate, and each species is on a different journey.

Other animal species also migrate, including insects, **amphibians**, reptiles, fish, and mammals. Migration is happening all the time: Herds of wildebeest arrive every January at green pastures in the southern Serengeti of Africa. Swarms of free-tailed bats arrive each March to caves in Texas. Northern fur seals gather on Alaskan islands each June. In September, Chinook salmon swim up rivers in Washington State. If you are in the right place at the right time, you can witness these amazing journeys. Yet, no matter where you live, you can see some birds migrating. In fact, much of what we know about migration comes from studying birds.

Aristotle, a naturalist and philosopher of ancient Greece, was one of the first to write about bird migration. He noted that cranes traveled from the mountains near Syria to the marshes along the Nile River in Egypt. He also wrote that pelicans, geese, swans, rails, doves, and many other birds flew to warmer regions to spend the winter.

DIVERSE JOURNEYS

Not all birds travel from north to south and back again: Some travel east to west. White-winged scoters are diving ducks. They can stay underwater for up to a minute to grab shellfish from the ocean floor. In the summer, they live near ponds and lakes in Alaska and western Canada. In the fall, they fly to milder conditions on the Pacific and Atlantic coasts, where there is less snow. Other migrants do not travel very far for a big difference

American robins have a partial migration, in which not all birds of the same species migrate. Some always stay in the South, while the others migrate from north to south in the winter.

in climate. Instead of going north or south, they travel up and down. Mountain birds, such as brindled titmice and mountain chickadees, migrate about 1,000 feet (305 meters) to lower elevations. They move from high-altitude evergreen forests to wooded valleys and streams.

Even within a bird species, some birds may migrate while others don't. This is called partial migration. Robins are a sign of spring's arrival in Northern states, because they migrate south during the cold winter months. But some robins live year-round in the South.

Some bird species migrate in one nonstop trip. Others stop along the way. Sea terns cannot rest for long on the water during their flights over oceans because they become waterlogged.

Sandhill cranes use the fertile wetlands along the Platte River as their layover spot during migration, where seeds and plants provide fuel for them to make the rest of their journey.

EXTREME BIRDS

With so many species traveling so many different routes, migrating birds cover every extreme.

Smallest: Hummingbirds, like the Rufous hummingbird, weigh about as much as a penny, but migrate 2,500 miles (4,000 kilometers) from southern Alaska to central Mexico.

Widest: The wandering albatross, with a wingspan of more than 10 feet (3 m), can travel for 10 months without touching land. The birds fly over the oceans around the South Pole for up to 12,500 miles (20,000 km). They rest while floating on the water.

Speediest: Most migrating birds travel between 19 miles per hour and 44 miles per hour (30 to 70 km per hour). The white-throated needle-tailed swift, which migrates from Siberia to Australia, can travel 106 miles (170 km) per hour—that's way over the speed limit on the highway.

Highest: The bar-headed goose regularly flies as high as 25,000 ft (9,000 m) on its migration across the Himalayan Mountains. Most people would become unconscious at this height, because there is so little oxygen in the air.

Longest nonstop flight: A bar-tailed godwit traveled for nine days straight, without landing or eating. It covered 7,145 miles (11,500 km) from Alaska to New Zealand. Biologists tracked the flight using a **satellite tag**. The bird flew an average of 34.8 miles (56 km) an hour. Along the way, the bird "slept" by shutting down one side of its brain at a time. It burned up its stores of fat, which made up more than half its body weight.

Longest journey measured: The sooty shearwater, a seabird about the weight of a baseball bat, flew nearly 40,000 miles (64,000 km) from its **breeding grounds** in New Zealand to its feeding grounds off the coasts of

An Arctic tern lives, on average, up to 30 years. They eat mainly fish and other small marine creatures as they make their long migratory journeys.

California, Alaska, and Japan, traveling as much as 565 miles (910 km) a day. Scientists believe that only the **Arctic** tern, which migrates between the Arctic and Antarctica, outdoes the sooty shearwater in distance traveled. However, scientists have not yet been able to track Arctic terns to measure the exact distances they fly.

Longest route: It is widely believed that the Arctic tern has the longest migration route of any animal in the world. It flies from the North Pole to the South Pole and back again. The perks? It sees more daylight hours during a year than any other living thing. That's because it spends the Northern hemisphere summer near the North Pole, and the Southern hemisphere summer near the South Pole.

For most birds, though, nonstop travel is unusual. It is much more common for birds to stop along the way to rest and refuel. Even a small cluster of bushes with berries can provide crucial energy for birds on the move. Birds may stay at stopover points for a few days or a few weeks, depending on how much energy they need. They might also wait for better weather or wind conditions for the next leg of their journey.

Some layover sites attract huge crowds of migratory birds. Favorite points in the United States include Hawk Mountain in Pennsylvania, where soaring **raptors** (such as golden eagles) congregate, and Delaware Bay, where migrating **shorebirds** gather to feed on the eggs of horseshoe crabs. A 75-mile (120-kilometer) stretch of the Platte River in Nebraska is a gathering spot for up to nine million birds each spring. They stop to feed in the fertile wetlands along the river. Almost all of the world's sandhill cranes—numbering about 500,000—spend about six weeks on the Platte River. Mostly, they eat corn, which quickly adds fat and gets them ready for the rest of their migration. Once the cranes have fed and rested, they continue their northward migration to Canada, Alaska, and Siberia.

Migrating birds may travel during the day, at night, or both. Ducks, geese, and swans travel during the day and at night. Some birds that travel during the day can feed while flying. Swallows and swifts, for example, feed on flying insects while they travel.

In contrast, most songbirds feed and rest during the day and travel at night. It is thought that cooler and less windy conditions at night make for better flying. Hidden in the night sky, the birds are almost invisible—except for all the chattering. Only when songbirds pass in front of the moon are they visible. In fact, moon watching is a way of counting how many migrants travel at night. During migration season, a moon watcher may see as many as 200 birds an hour.

TRACKING TRAVELERS: RADARS, RADIOS, AND RINGS

There are many ways to learn about migratory birds besides moon watching. Since the 1960s, scientists have used radar to track migratory birds. Radar images can reveal the surprising

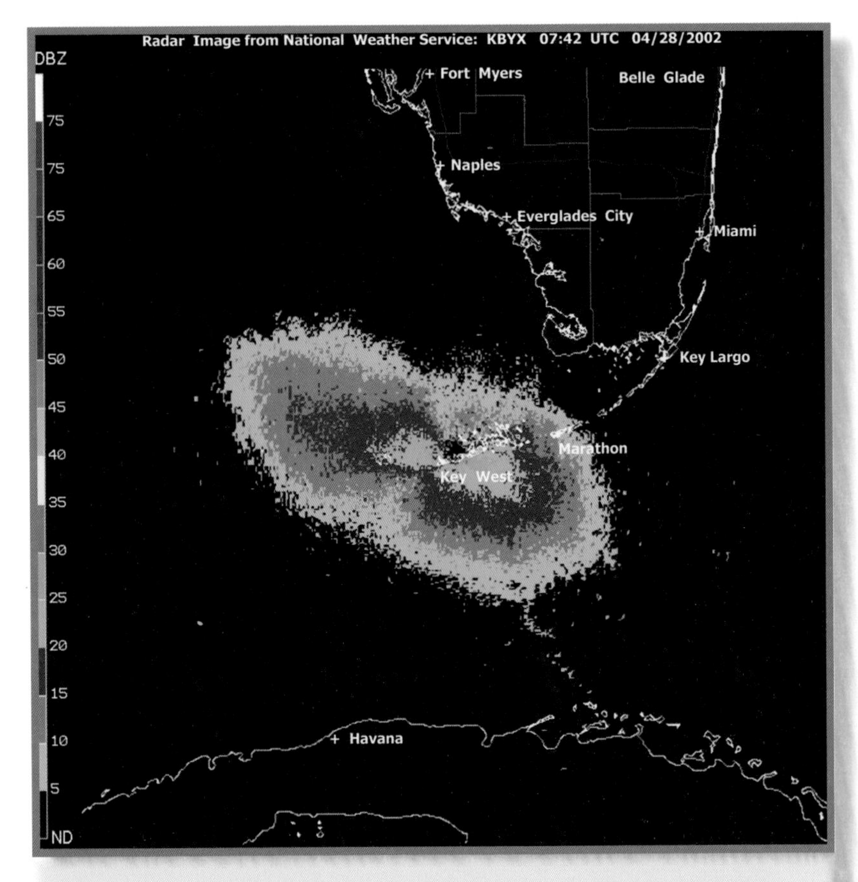

This Doppler radar image shows a large flock of birds (blue and green areas) migrating over Key West, Florida. The dark green area shows the densest part of the flock, which is believed to contain 6,250 birds per square kilometer. Land and shorebirds migrate through Key West from wintering grounds in the tropics to summer areas in North America.

number of birds taking flight in the night skies, as well as their speed, altitude, and flight path.

The most common method of studying migratory birds is banding. Ornithologists, people who study birds, trap them on the move using fine nets called mist nets. Without harming the

A band was placed on this gray catbird's right leg. Banding is used to track migratory birds.

birds, they carefully remove each bird from the net and place a band or metal ring around its leg. The ring has a unique serial number, as well as a telephone number to call if the band is found. Bands come in different sizes. Systematic banding began around 1900. In North America, the U.S. Fish and Wildlife Service and the Canadian Wildlife Service regulate banding. They keep track of all birds that are banded and record where each banded bird is recovered. For small birds, on average, 1 of every 300 banded birds is recaptured at some point. For larger birds, the recapture rate is much higher: 1 in 10.

Barn swallows were one of the first bird species to be extensively banded. Researchers have built an amazing picture of the species' journey from birds found with bands. Barn swallows travel 6,000 miles (10,000 km) from England to South Africa. They fly over the English Channel, through the Pyrenees Mountains in France, across the Mediterranean Sea, across the Sahara desert, through tropical storms, and over the rainforests of Zaire. Four months after leaving England, they reach South Africa. It's a treacherous journey. About half of adult barn swallows survive and return to England. Only 20% of young birds who make the voyage for the first time survive the trip to South Africa and back.

Satellite and different forms of radio transmitters are the most recent advances in bird tracking. A transmitter is a small device attached to the bird. It transmits a signal to a radio or a satellite. This allows researchers to pinpoint a bird's location in real time. These kinds of tags provided the first measurements of actual distances traveled by migratory birds.

Some tracking devices have to be as clever and durable as the birds with which they travel. Albatrosses can spend months, if not years, on the open sea. To track these birds, scientists developed a tag called a light-level logger. Designed to last more than three years, it measures the amount of daylight over time. This gives scientists information about the dawn and dusk of each day in an albatross's life. With this information, they can figure out a bird's location within about 100 miles (160 km). Scientists found that in one year, some albatrosses travel all the way around the world at least twice.

WHY GO SO FAR?

A migrant faces many dangers along the way. A safe homecoming is not guaranteed. Yet, the need for food is a major reason birds and other animals migrate south each fall in North America. During winter, the ground is covered in snow and insects and fruits are scarce. There is not enough food for most birds to survive. On the other hand, in warmer climates, birds need less energy to stay warm.

Still, they can't stay in milder climates all year long because other birds and animals live in the warmer areas, too. Food and nest-building space can become scarce when **breeding** season starts. It takes energy and space to fight for a mate, build a nest, lay eggs, and raise young. If a species is spread out over an area, there is less competition for food and space. When North American migrants move from their sunny wintering grounds in Mexico, Central America, and the Caribbean Islands, they return to an area eight times larger where there is less competition.

When to begin the journey depends on a mixture of cues. The changing length of daylight is one key signal. Shortening days in the fall indicate that it is time for southern migrations. Lengthening days in the spring mean it is time to head north again. The change in daylight coincides with changes inside an animal's body. Changes happen in an animal's levels of hormones: chemicals that help regulate weight gain and reproduction.

Daylight and hormones may tell a bird the general month or week to leave, and weather can help determine the day that a flock of birds will take flight. Birds often time their departures to meet up with favorable winds. These winds will give them an extra boost in the right direction. Birds know when a cold front is coming. They will start flying before it arrives. On a night with clear skies and winds headed in the right direction, waves of migrating birds may fill the sky.

Even without any visible cues of changes in day length, food shortages, or dropping temperatures, birds are driven to travel. They instinctively know when, where, and how long to fly. Experiments with birds kept in cages show that they have something called **migratory restlessness**. At certain times of the year they will hop and flutter in the cage. They're not moving randomly. They are trying to fly in a particular direction. They will continue this behavior for as long as it would take them to get to their destination in the wild. Birds kept under artificial lighting that does not change throughout the year still show migratory restlessness. They seem to have a built-in alarm clock that tells them it is time to go.

Migratory restlessness shows that migration is a very strong instinct. It is something birds are born understanding they must do. Although birds might fine-tune their behavior in response to daylight, a warm spring, or food availability, the plan to migrate is hard-wired.

Even the direction in which a bird travels is inherited from its parents. Researchers in Germany mated birds from two different **populations** of blackcap warblers. Each fall, German blackcaps fly southwest, spending the winter in the western Mediterranean. Austrian blackcaps, on the other hand, fly southeast to the eastern Mediterranean, and then on to eastern Africa. The offspring of these two bird populations showed migratory restlessness, hopping and fluttering directly southward—halfway between the directions taken by their parents.

PACKING FOR THE TRIP

To understand how difficult it is to migrate, consider this: A marathon runner weighs an average of 139 pounds (63 kg) and runs 26.2 miles (42 km) without stopping. In contrast, a migrating Canada goose weighs just 14 pounds (6.4 kg) but can fly 600 miles (966 km) without stopping. For the marathon runner to make the same journey relative to his or her weight, he or she would have to go almost 6,000 miles. That's 225 marathons in a row. It's like running from New York City to Los Angeles and back again without stopping.

To pack enough energy for such an intense trip, many migrating birds gorge on food before they leave. They store the extra energy in a fat layer just below their skin. Fat is a low-weight, high-power fuel. For a half-ounce (15 g) bird, one-thirteenth of an ounce (1 g) of fat can power a 125-mile (200-km) flight. Depending on the length of the flight, a bird may gain 15% to 100% of its body weight before migrating. Every ounce of fat can make a difference. A hummingbird may double its weight (to become about as heavy as four paperclips) before it begins its nonstop flight across the Gulf of Mexico.

The migration of the red knot is an incredible story of energy gained and lost. This shorebird begins by stuffing itself along the southeastern shores of South America. It eats small mussels in Argentina's tide pools. Further north, it consumes snails from grassy lagoons in southern Brazil. Well-fueled for the first leg of its trip, the red knot makes a three-day nonstop flight of 2,300 miles (3,700 km) over the Brazilian rainforest. Then, along the northeast shore of Brazil, it feasts on mussels in the roots of mangrove forests. In just four days, it travels 4,000 miles (6,500 km) to the Delaware Bay, which sits between Delaware and New Jersey. Along the way, it uses all of its body fat for energy. On the shores of the bay, it eats as many horseshoe crab eggs as it can. Less than two weeks later, it undertakes another non-stop flight of almost 1,800 miles (3,000 km). This trip ends in the chilly **tundra** of northern Canada.

It's hard to believe, but a female red knot still has enough energy left to mate and lay eggs that add up to half of her body weight. The return flight of the red knot follows the same pattern of feasting in between long flights. After 9 months, almost 20,000 miles, and a lot of energy, red knots will be back at the southern tip of South America.

Before its epic journey, a red knot will feast so it can store body fat for energy.

TAKING FLIGHT: SOARING, FLAPPING, AND BOUNDING

With their light, hollow bones and feathered wings, birds are made for long-distance air travel. Yet, not all birds fly the same way. Continuous flapping takes the most energy. Birds with relatively small wings for their large weight, such as ducks and geese, use this method. While migrating, these birds need to stop often to rest and feed. These birds also tend to fly in a *V*-shaped formation. This formation creates the best air movement for efficient flying. A flock of 25 birds in a *V*-formation can fly as much as 70% farther than a bird flying by itself. The leader and the birds at the tip of the *V* work the hardest. Because of that, the birds will rotate in and out of these positions.

Soaring uses the least energy. Birds with wide wingspans, such as cranes, storks, and raptors, fly this way. Soaring harnesses the power of rising air. Air rises when it is heated above some areas of land. It also rises when it meets an obstruction, such as a mountain range. Raptors will migrate along mountain ridges, where the air acts as a series of rising elevators. A raptor will effortlessly spiral up with the rising air. When it reaches the top, it will glide down to the next "air elevator" and rise again, moving forward. Soaring is so energy efficient that a raptor, such as the Swainson's hawk, can fly 5,000 miles (8,000 km) from New Mexico to Argentina without stopping to feed.

Most birds do something in between soaring and constant flapping. Medium-sized birds will flap and then glide, with wings outstretched. Smaller birds, on the other hand, use bounding flight: They take short breaks from flapping, tucking in their wings for a bit. Because flapping takes energy, these birds use winds to migrate long distances. For example, the blackpoll warbler, which is only about 4 inches (10 cm) long, flies nonstop over water from the northeast coast of the United

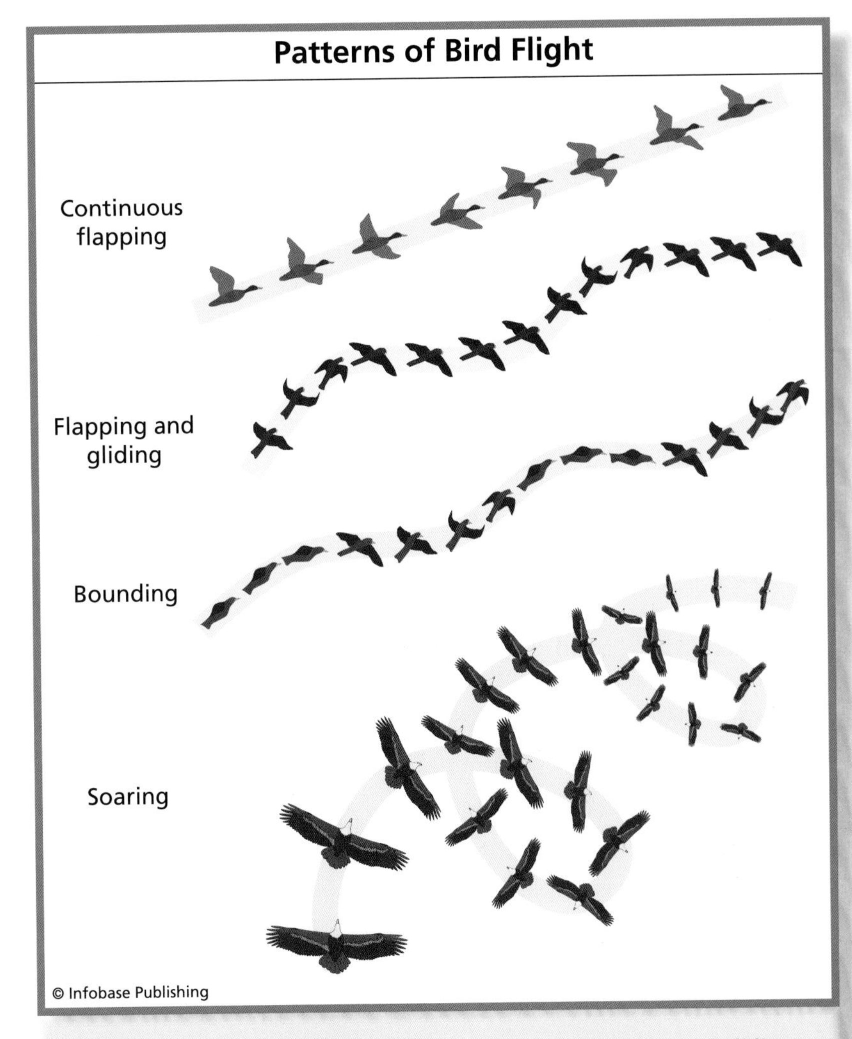

Patterns of bird flight include continuous flapping, flapping and gliding, bounding, and soaring. Soaring makes use of the friction of wind over water; soarers—who have long and thin wings that they keep firmly outstretched—will fly up into the wind and then glide with it.

States to South America in just five days. The bird waits for strong northwest winds. The winds carry it out to sea, across the western Atlantic, and to the northern coast of South America. Yet, even with this extra nudge from the wind, a blackpoll warbler will flap its wings as many as four million times during the journey.

SKILLED PILOTS WITHOUT A PLANE

If people were dropped into the middle of an unknown forest and told to find their way home, they would have a difficult time. They would need some extra information: where the forest was in relation to home and which way was north. Even then, they might not be able to get home. Birds are different: A Manx shearwater was taken from its nest in England and dropped off 3,000 miles away in Massachusetts. Amazingly, 12 days later, it was back in its very own nest.

White-crowned sparrows have similar powers of **navigation**. Researchers caught 30 of these birds midway through their migration from Alaska to their winter homes in the southwestern United States. The birds were flown across the country in the windowless pet compartments of commercial jets. They were taken from Seattle, Washington, to New Jersey, approximately 2,200 miles (3,700 km) east. A few days later, the birds were released. Each had a radio transmitter attached to a piece of cotton, which was glued between its shoulders. Researchers followed the birds' flight paths. They found that the 15 adult birds realized they needed to fly southwest to get to the nesting grounds. The 15 juveniles, who had never made the trip before, however, continued to fly south.

Scientists have long been puzzled over how migratory birds are able to find sites so far away. Yet, millions of migrating birds manage to find their way from summer to winter homes and back again. In the case of the white-crowned sparrows, the fact that the adults were able to correct their route after such a huge diversion suggests the birds may build navigational maps in their minds as they migrate.

For migrating birds, navigation means knowing where they want to go, where they are relative to that destination, and which direction to fly to get there. Reaching a destination is not as simple as flying in a straight line. Birds need to compensate for how winds or storms change their path, and they may need to take an indirect route to stop at feeding grounds, or to avoid long crosses over deserts or water. A pilot would use maps, a compass, calculations, and a variety of devices that measure speed and height to reach his or her destination, but a bird has navigational tools.

With a "bird's-eye view" of the world as they travel, some birds can use landmarks, such as mountains or bodies of water, to guide them home. However, landmarks are much less important to bird navigation than other cues that are less obvious to humans. These include the sun, stars, smells, sounds, and Earth's **magnetic field**.

Birds can use the position of the sun in the sky to orient themselves. They seem to know that the sun is in the east in the morning, and the west in the afternoon. Using the sun as a compass means that birds also have a sense of time. Birds do seem to have an internal clock. To understand if the clock was important for migration, researchers kept **homing** pigeons under artificial lighting for several days. The lights went on six hours before actual sunrise and went off six hours before actual sunset. This shifted the birds' internal clocks by six hours: When it was 6 AM, for example, the birds thought it was noon. When the birds were released at 9 AM, they flew in the wrong direction to get home. According to their internal clock, it was six hours later, or 3 PM Therefore, they flew the direction that made sense for an afternoon position of the sun.

Birds that migrate at night rely on the positions of the stars. The North Star, or Polaris, provides a fixed point in the sky that shows which direction is north. Birds even use constellations to navigate. Researchers studied migration restlessness movements

Researchers theorize that white-crowned sparrows create navigational maps as they migrate.

of captive birds in a planetarium. By changing the positions of the "stars" in the sky, they could change the direction in which the birds wanted to fly.

Smells and sounds also may help a bird find its way around. Smells are probably most important for short distances. They may help a bird find its nest once it is in the right area. Shearwaters and petrels are seabirds. Their sharp sense of smell helps them find their nests, which are marked by a musky odor. Homing pigeons also use smell to return home. When a homing pigeon's sense of smell is disrupted, it cannot find its way home.

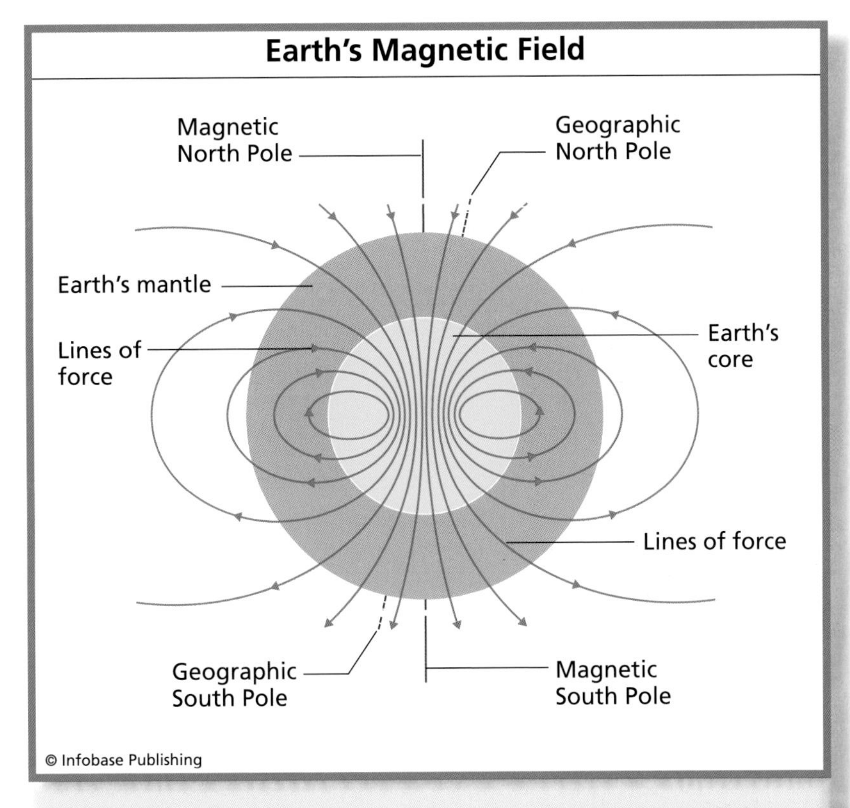

Birds use Earth's magnetic field—north and south poles linked by lines of magnetic force—in order to navigate during migration. They also have bits of magnetite in their brain, which is like having a built-in compass.

This suggests that pigeons create "odor maps" of the areas they fly over and use them to navigate.

Some researchers believe that birds listen to sounds along the way. This gives them another way to orient themselves. They can hear waves on shores, wind on mountain ranges, the sounds of other birds gathering in good flight areas or feeding areas, or even the calls of frogs from a marsh.

Perhaps the most important navigational tool for migrating birds is a sense of Earth's magnetic field. Although it is not visible, a magnetic field surrounds the planet. Iron deep below

CAN HUMANS SENSE EARTH'S MAGNETIC FIELD?

Magnetite has been found in the brains or bodies of many migratory animals, including honeybees, birds, monarch butterflies, sea turtles, and fish. Humans also have magnetite in their brains. A thimbleful of human brain tissue contains about five million pin-shaped magnetic crystals. The link between these crystals in humans and navigation is still unknown.

In the 1980s, a series of experiments by the biologist Robin Baker created quite a stir. People were blindfolded and taken on a bus to an unknown location. Then, they were asked to point toward where they started. Those who had bar magnets placed in their blindfolds seemed to have a disrupted sense of direction. They were much less likely to point in the right direction, compared with people who did not have magnets near their heads. Later studies did not get the same results. It is still unclear whether humans can sense Earth's magnetic field.

Humans who are exceptional navigators might shed light on this mystery. Throughout history, some Pacific Islanders sailed hundreds of miles over open ocean without even a compass. Anthropologists have found they used different kinds of information to find their way, including the position of key stars and the sun, the speed and direction of waves, and signs of land, such as cloud formations and land-nesting birds. But there may be more. Some of these navigators say that when they get stuck in areas with overcast skies, darkness, and still waters, something else seems to kick in. They just "know" where to go. One described it as turning his head in circles until he had a feeling that he was headed the right way. And he was.

the surface makes the planet behave like a giant bar magnet, with poles at the north and the south and magnetic lines connecting them. This is what makes a needle in a compass point toward north. Researchers have placed small magnets on birds. This disrupts their ability to sense this magnetic field. In the late 1970s, researchers discovered that birds' brains contain bits of **magnetite**, a magnetic kind of iron that acts much like a needle in a compass. Having magnetite in the brain is like having a built-in compass.

The magnetite may also provide birds with a magnetic map of the globe. Scientists have long suspected birds' eyes contain certain chemicals that sense or even see Earth's magnetic field. Biologists have found that these chemicals are linked to an area of the brain that processes visual information. The biologists believe the magnetic field or magnetic direction may be perceived as a dark or light spot in the normal visual field of the bird. When the bird turns its head, the field moves.

2

Swimmers: Hungry Whales and Other Ocean Travelers

THE SKY IS a common way to migrate, but the oceans of the world also are home to marathon migrations. Oceans cover more than 70% of Earth's surface. On average, they are more than 2 miles (3.2 km) deep. If the world's highest mountain, Mount Everest, was on the bottom of the ocean, it would be completely covered by water.

Unlike the sky, the ocean is a migration highway that is mostly hidden from our view. Yet, researchers are beginning to learn more about the journeys made by underwater animals. Some of these animals are as small as the head of a pin. Others, such as the blue whale, weigh more than 25 elephants. They migrate to be in a better place to eat, reproduce, or find safety.

The smallest migratory swimmers are animals known as **zooplankton**. They range from less than one inch long (2 cm) to eight inches long (20 cm). These tiny water creatures usually move with the currents, but they also are capable of swimming. Zooplankton do not migrate in the more familiar annual north-south trips. Instead, their migration happens every day. They

GETTING E-MAIL FROM A SHARK

Seeing the migration of an underwater species is tricky. In April 2005, however, the water off the coast of southern Florida was so clear that people could watch hundreds of blacktip sharks and Spinner sharks on their annual spring migration north to North Carolina. Some of the sharks were only 10 feet offshore. This vivid view of underwater migration is rare. Fish and whales can be tagged, similar to banding birds. If they are recaptured, researchers can find out where they traveled. Unique markings, such as the markings on whales' flukes (the two end lobes of its tail), are used like fingerprints to identify them. Still, neither of these techniques works well for most other ocean animals, which are hard to find a second time.

A breakthrough in tracking technology came with the development of radio and satellite tags. These tags relay

(continues)

Tags help scientists track these scalloped hammerhead sharks off the Galapagos Islands in the Pacific Ocean as they migrate north.

(continued)

information about an animal's position to a receiver, such as a radio or an orbiting satellite. These tags are small enough to fit in one hand. They provide incredible amounts of information about migrating whales, sharks, sea turtles, tuna, seals, squid, and even seabirds.

Different tags work for different uses. A Smart Position-Only Tag (SPOT) sends constant information about an animal's position, as well as its speed and the water temperature. People can watch a tagged animal move across oceans in real time on a Web browser. (See, for example, http://www.topp.org/.) These tags work well for animals that spend time near the surface. The tag turns off when the animal goes underwater. This helps the battery last longer (one battery can last two years).

A Pop-up Archival Tag (PAT) collects information but does not transmit until the tag releases from the animal. The tag releases on its own either 30 or 90 days after it is attached. After it releases, it floats to the surface. These tags work well for animals that spend most of their time under water. A PAT tag can reveal where an animal was since it was tagged. It also provides information on the depth and temperature of the water through which it traveled. The information is sent by email to the researcher who attached the tag.

This information helps scientists understand and appreciate these mysterious migrating animals. It also helps to protect these creatures. Knowing how deep whales dive can help keep them safe from the gear and netting that are used to catch fish. If people know where animals are, they can avoid human activities in those areas, such as underwater military training activities and oil and gas drilling. Tracking of sea turtles has revealed underwater "turtle highways." These are commonly traveled routes that fishing boats could avoid.

migrate up and down, like an elevator in the ocean. This is called **vertical migration**.

Vertical migration may be the largest movement of animals on Earth because it involves so many creatures and happens in almost all oceans and lakes. Around sunrise, zooplankton sink. At sunset, they rise toward the water's surface. For something so tiny to swim through ocean water takes a great deal of energy. To zooplankton, the water is as thick as molasses. Yet, they must do it because their food source (phytoplankton, or tiny plants, like algae) is at the surface, so they go there at night to eat. During

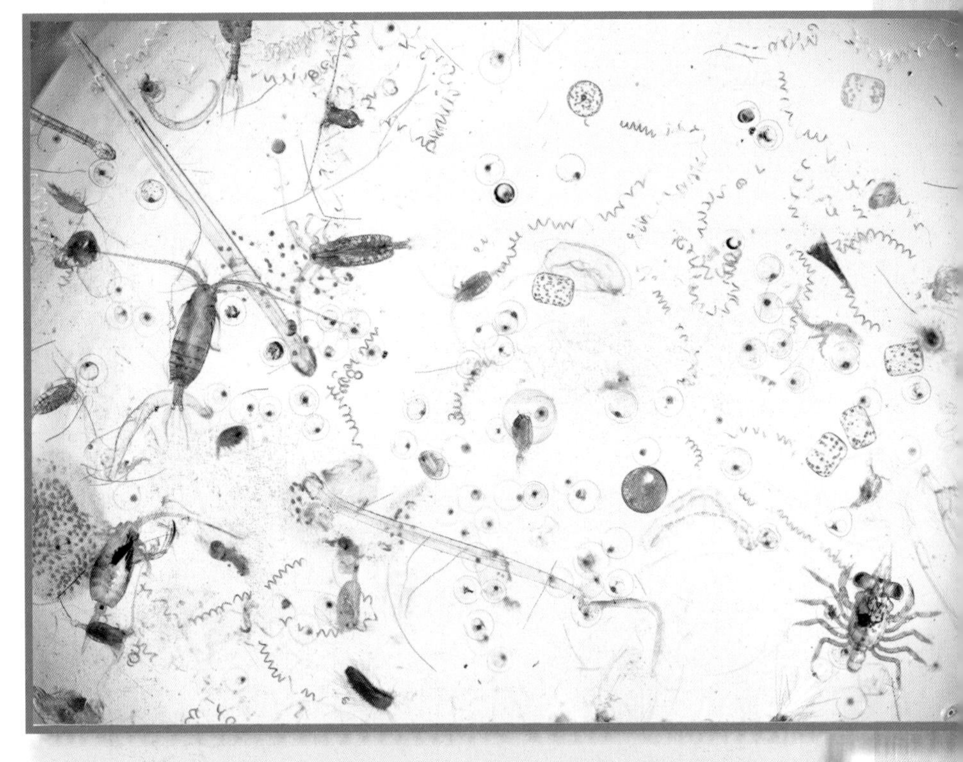

This magnified image of a drop of seawater shows it to be filled with life. Zooplankton are the smallest migratory swimmers; they migrate up and down in a process called vertical migration. They sink at sunrise to escape predators and keep cool, and then they rise at sunset to get to their food source at the surface.

the day, when **predators** can see them, zooplankton retreat to deeper waters to hide and keep cool. These little creatures will travel 300 feet to 3,000 feet (91 m to 914 m) per day. This would be similar to a person walking 50 miles (80 km) a day.

Many fish also migrate. Some make daily vertical migrations, like zooplankton. Swordfish and sand tiger sharks rise to the surface to feed at night, but disappear to deeper waters during the day. Young sockeye salmon stay at about 250 feet deep (76 m) during the day, but rise to about 30 feet (9 m) at night to avoid predation from other fish.

Other fish travel long distances across the ocean. Species of tuna occupy all the major oceans of the world. Like many other ocean migrants, tuna feed in cold waters and move to warm waters to **spawn**. In the warm waters, the fish release their eggs and sperm. North Atlantic bluefin tuna follow a circular route. They tend to swim with the Atlantic Ocean currents, in a clockwise direction. They breed in the warm waters of the Gulf of Mexico. Then they head north, past Florida, in search of better feeding waters along the New England and Canadian coasts. They may cross the Atlantic Ocean and swim along the coasts of Scandinavia, into the Mediterranean Sea. To return to spawn in the Gulf of Mexico, they must cross the Atlantic Ocean. Some tuna complete this transoceanic roundtrip every year. These fish can "sprint" as fast as 50 miles (80 km) per hour, and can cruise 5 to 10 miles per hour (8 to 16 km/hr) without resting.

Great white sharks are the world's largest predatory fish. Until recently, scientists believed that these sharks spent most of their lives close to shore, feeding on seals and sea lions. But recent advances in tracking have revealed that great whites migrate. Sharks tracked from the coast of central California swam along the northern coast in the fall. But in winter, they headed out into the Pacific Ocean. Some traveled as far west as Hawaii, 2,800 miles (4,500 km) away.

Scientists now know that great white sharks migrate rather than just stay close to the shore or roam aimlessly. Some researchers believe they may use visual clues, such as the location of the sun and the moon, to navigate.

A great white made the fastest swimming migration ever recorded. Tracked with a satellite transmitter, the shark traveled across the Indian Ocean, from South Africa to Australia and back in nine months. That's a journey of 13,400 miles (more than 20,000 km). It completed the one-way trip of 6,800 miles (11,100 km) in 99 days. Robert Hueter, director of the Center for Shark Research at the Mote Marine Laboratory in Sarasota, Florida, said that the discovery advances shark biology. It shows that sharks are not "ocean nomads that roam about aimlessly." Researchers still don't know why great white sharks migrate so far from their coastal feeding grounds. They might do it so they can mate with unrelated great white sharks, but no one knows for sure.

How did this shark—named Nicole by researchers—know where she was going? What led her back to the same bay in which she was originally tagged? Sharks are sensitive to dim light. Some researchers think they may use visual cues, such as the location of the sun or moon, to navigate. Data from Nicole's tag show that she spent more than 60% of her time swimming at the surface, and swam in a straight line.

Swimming migrations are not limited to aquatic animals. Penguins also migrate by swimming. Most penguins migrate through the ocean for many months, feeding. They return to land only to breed. Penguins are difficult to track in the water, so it isn't clear where they swim. Some appear to stay close to breeding grounds, while other species venture at least as far as 600 miles (1,000 km) from land.

AWARD-WINNING WHALES

Whales are one group of migratory swimmers that are hard to miss—and not only because of their size. Many whales—including humpback, blue, gray, and right whales—swim from icy waters near the poles to warm waters near the equator. The blue whale is the largest animal on Earth. This mammal can be 100 feet (30 m) long and weigh more than 120 tons (100 tonnes). Its tongue weighs more than a car.

Humpback whales are the longest known travelers of any mammal. Each winter, humpback whales travel from the Antarctic to the northern tropics to find warm water in which to raise their young. Seven humpback whales were tracked from Antarctica to Costa Rica, a swim of 5,160 miles (8,300 km). One mother and her calf made the trip in 161 days.

Gray whales also make long journeys. They travel from Arctic waters to the Mexican coast. The roundtrip distance can be as much as 12,000 miles (20,000 km). By the time a gray whale is 50 years old, it will have swum enough miles to travel to the moon and back again. A gray whale takes its first journey before it is seven months old. Along the way, whales face injury by the propellers of ships near busy coastal ports, entanglement in steel and rope fishing gear, attacks by orcas, and starvation.

For about five months out of the year, the gray whale lives north of Alaska, in the Bering and Chukchi seas. The whales live in an area about as big as Maryland and Delaware combined. In the summer, the area has nearly 24 hours of daylight. The cold waters also are rich in nutrients, so food here is plentiful. In the fall, daylight decreases, temperatures drop, and the gray whale begins its migration. It will travel south nonstop for 55 days. Although there is much less food off the coast of Mexico, pregnant females must make the journey. Their calves would not survive in the cold waters of the Arctic. Males and non-pregnant females also head south to mate. Whales that are too young to mate still will make the trip. Perhaps they are learning from experience by traveling with the group. All whales will spend seven months away from their Arctic home, eating almost nothing the entire time. Imagine a pregnant woman running marathons, then giving birth and feeding her young, all on an empty stomach.

By January, gray whales reach the warm lagoons off the coast of Mexico. Here, pregnant females give birth to 15-foot (4.6-m) calves. Other females will mate; their offspring will be born on the next trip south. The calves' six-month stay in the lagoons is training time. Young whales strengthen their flukes and flippers. They also learn the rhythm of diving: swimming underwater for three to five minutes, surfacing to blow and breathe, and

Gray whales make long migrations to the coast of Mexico, where for seven months they barely eat. During this time, pregnant gray whales must travel, give birth, and feed their young.

diving again, all while taking into account the current and waves. Mothers are protective of their calves during this time. They stay close, preventing the calves from being swept out to sea by strong tidal currents. Winter also is a time for the calves to turn milk into blubber. Though the older whales have little to eat, a calf will drink a hundred gallons of its mother's milk per day. The milk is nearly 50% fat, and the calves grow rapidly.

In the spring, ready to eat, the whales will begin to turn northward again. The newly pregnant females will leave first, followed by the males and other young whales. The mothers with their young calves will leave last. This gives the calves as much time as possible to bulk up for the trip. Spring is a key season for whale watchers to see this journey along the California coast. Amazingly, these animals that were once hunted to the brink of **extinction** appear friendly to humans.

The journey home is challenging. The whales are on their last energy reserves, and some are caring for inexperienced young. Calves are vulnerable to attacks from orcas (killer whales) along the way. The very old and the very young may not migrate all the way to the Arctic. They may go only as far as the coast of northern California or southern Alaska. Some whales have quit migrating and live in these areas all year, but these whales make up less than 2% of all gray whales.

When the whales arrive at their summer feeding grounds, they will have lost one-third of their pre-migration weight. Some whales will not make it. Those that do will feast again, filtering amphipods and **krill** (shrimp-like creatures) through baleen (fringe-like plates in the upper jaw). This will be their first good meal after almost seven months and 10,000 miles (16,000 km) or more of swimming.

NAVIGATING UNDERWATER

Researchers know much more about migratory fliers than they do about swimmers. It seems that swimmers use a variety of tools, just as birds do. The ocean floor is as textured and varied as the land above water. Swimmers may be able to use some of their senses to follow landmarks, such as underwater mountains and valleys, but it is difficult to see through miles of water. This is where sound comes in handy. Water conducts sound better than air, and whales can hear much better than humans. For some whales, this fine-tuned ability helps them see. Toothed whales, such as sperm whales, use sound, rather than light, to "see" the world around them. This sound-based method to picture the ocean landscape is called **echolocation**. Sound bounces off surfaces and returns as an echo with information about that object's distance and size. Sperm whales, for example, emit a series of

THE NOISY OCEAN

The ocean is a noisy place, and it's becoming noisier. Imagine trying to hear someone's voice across the room over a blaring radio, a blender, and two trumpet players. That is what whales are experiencing in the ocean. For days or weeks at a time, oil prospectors will blast compressed air on the sea floor, looking for oil or gas reserves. The U.S. Navy uses sonar to detect and communicate with submarines and other ocean vessels. Sonar is low-frequency sound, much like what a whale can hear but much louder. To a whale, sonar can sound like a rifle going off repeatedly, at close range. Add in the regular traffic of large ships, and the combined noise can make it nearly impossible for whales to use sound.

Each year, whales and dolphins swim onto shores and are stranded. Many of them die. Sometimes, groups of 10, or sometimes more than 100, whales or dolphins are beached at once. Strandings occur worldwide. The National Marine Fisheries Service reported that in the United States between 1990 and 2000, about 3,600 animals were stranded each year. There are several explanations. Some relate to navigation.

Strandings seem more common in areas with gently sloping beaches or especially sandy coasts. Echolocation may not work as well in these areas. According to another idea, mass beachings happen because undersea animals are exposed to pressure changes during an undersea earthquake. The pressure changes would cause ear injuries that weaken the ability to navigate. Other scientists have found clicks during their dives. Regular clicks function as long-range sonar. Sometimes the clicks are so close together that they sound like a continuous buzz.

Scientists have come up with several reasons for why whales (*as shown here*) and dolphins have trouble navigating and wash up ashore, including ear damage that undersea earthquakes and the Navy's use of sonar can cause.

that whales, in particular, may get thrown off course in areas where, because of local geology, Earth's magnetic field is distorted or even reversed.

Strandings have increased in recent years. Scientists are linking the increase in the problem to the Navy's use of sonar. They say that the intense blasts of sound created by the Navy's powerful sonar system either directly injure whales and dolphins or distress them into surfacing so quickly that the pressure change damages their ears. Then, disoriented, they can end up on shore.

This orca whale is "spy hopping" by pushing up so that its eyes are just above water, and then slipping back down again.

Another navigational tool a swimmer may use is magnetite. Magnetite acts like a built-in compass and has been found in the brains of fish, like salmon and tuna, as well as whales. Cetaceans (the animal family to which whales belong) also have magnetite in their eyes, where it may function in the same way. Like birds, swimmers with little information about their surroundings might use Earth's magnetic fields to direct them, but they might also use information about the world above water.

Whales and some sharks have been known to "spy hop." They push their bodies up so their eyes are just above water, and then slip back down. It seems that the animals are taking a look around. Maybe they are collecting information about the shore or the position of the sun or moon.

3

Walkers: Millions of Feet, Claws, and Hooves on the Move

BIRDS, BATS, AND INSECTS fly long distances, sometimes crossing continents or oceans. Swimming animals frequently migrate halfway across the world. Sometimes, these migrants can rely on a little help from their surroundings. Birds can fly in the same direction as strong winds, or glide on rising air. Fish and whales may swim in the "highways" created by ocean currents. Yet, many other animals migrate by walking. They often do not travel as many miles as fliers or swimmers, but walking migrants must always rely on their own energy to put one foot (or paw or hoof) in front of the other.

These migrants also offer the most spectacular opportunities to see animals in motion. People usually can't witness underwater journeys or birds flying in the night, but they can watch herds of animals crossing mountains, rivers, and tracts of land.

Many animals migrate by walking. Some birds even migrate this way. Ostriches and emus travel long distances over land. Emperor penguins do, too. Amphibians travel because their lives are split between land and water. Each spring, frogs, toads, salamanders, and newts will make migrations from their land homes, usually in forests, to ponds or streams. There, they breed and lay eggs. These are migrations of a few miles, at most. Sometimes they go unnoticed, but sometimes amphibians travel in such large numbers that they carpet the ground.

Hoofed animals make some of the most spectacular long-distance walks. These include elk, pronghorns, gazelles, and other deer and antelope. Each year, more than one million wildebeest take part in the largest walking migration near the equator in Africa. A wildebeest is a 400-pound (181-kg) antelope with a white beard and heavy curved horns. The longest migration happens much farther north, near the North Pole. There, herds of reindeer—also known as caribou—travel farther than any other walker, and they do it under brutally cold conditions.

THE WILDEBEEST OF THE SERENGETI

To the Masai people who live here, *Serengeti* means "the endless plains that go up to the sky." The Serengeti is an 11,500-square-mile (30,000-square-kilometer) open plain that stretches across Tanzania and Kenya. This African landscape is ever changing. When the rains come, it shifts from barren to fertile. From a towering black cloud, a raindrop falls on the dry Serengeti plains. Within seconds, torrents of rain shower the land. Within a day or two, the dusty ground and withered plants transform into vibrant grasslands.

Each year, nearly two million animals follow a roughly clockwise path within the Serengeti. More than one million wildebeest, together with 500,000 zebras and Thomson's gazelles, migrate as many as 2,000 miles (3,000 km) in search of fresh grass. The drive for food is strong. The herds wander through

Some wildebeest and zebras stand together near the Mara River in Africa. They, along with Thomson's gazelles, migrate through the Serengeti every year.

drought-stricken grasslands, climb along rocky gorges, and cross crocodile-infested rivers.

The ground trembles when the animals gallop across the plains. Their hoofbeats—together with the grunts of wildebeest and the brays and snorts of zebra—make up the sound of migration in the Serengeti.

The cycle starts in December or January, when rain falls in the southern Serengeti. The herds will spend three to five months moving within this rich southern feeding ground. They follow the rains to find nutrient- and moisture-rich tender green blades of grass. More than 500 animals per square mile (200 per sq km) crowd together for the feast. In fact, wildebeest live in the densest concentrations of any large mammal, except for humans. During this time, wildebeest also give birth to young in spectacular numbers: 300,000 calves can be born within three weeks. The young wildebeest calves are adapted to life on the move. They can run just minutes after they are born. After about two days, the calves are so hard to catch that the spotted hyenas, the main wildebeest predator, seldom bother with them. Within three days, the young calves can keep up with the herd.

In May, the southern plains begin to dry out. The herds, new calves included, gradually move north and west to find more grass. By June, the dry season has set in. Water is not plentiful, and most of the green is gone. Many animals die during this time, some from exhaustion.

During the dry season, wildebeest move into woodlands, which have more dependable water sources. There, they begin mating. Thousands of territorial bulls (male wildebeest) round up the cows (female wildebeest). Each male tries to breed with as many females as possible. These animals breed in one massive **synchronized** event, which happens around a full moon. Approximately 90% of all females become pregnant. About eight months later, all of the calves are born at about the same time.

Trudging north, many wildebeest will reach the northern grassy plains of the Serengeti. There they will graze through September and October. Then, as dark clouds gather in the south, it is time to move on again to greener pastures. By November,

SERENGETI'S NEW RIVAL

Nearly 25 years of civil war have squelched most wildlife research in southern Sudan. When researchers conducted the first aerial survey of the area since the war began, it revealed some big surprises. The 2007 survey found large migrating herds that may rival those of the Serengeti plains, according to the Wildlife Conservation Society.

Southern Sudan covers an area of about 225,000 square miles (582,747 sq km). It sits between the Sahara Desert and Africa's belt of tropical forests. Wildlife biologists have long known that its grasslands, woodlands, and swamps were home to elephants, zebras, giraffes, and other animals. Before the civil war, an estimated 900,000 white-eared kob (a kind of antelope) had been seen migrating there. But in 1983, war broke out. Historically, wars have often meant a death sentence for wildlife. As environmental protections collapse, poachers sweep in to kill animals for meat, horn, and ivory. People shoot game to feed themselves.

Yet, that doesn't seem to be the case for much of the wildlife in southern Sudan. Herds of more than one million gazelles and antelope may be larger than the Serengeti's herds of wildebeest. The researchers saw white-eared kob joined by hundreds of thousands of mongalla gazelles and tiang, a species of antelope. They formed a solid column of animals 30 miles (42 km) across and 50 miles (81 km) long. The biologists estimate there were 1.3 million kob, tiang, and gazelle in their survey area alone.

the herds will begin to complete their trip, moving southward. Sometimes a line of moving animals can be 1,000 miles (1,600 km) long.

No one wildebeest leads the herd in this migration. They may follow each other, but who travels at the front can change from day to day, or moment to moment. When a predator, such as a lion, scatters the herd, a new animal may take the lead. Wildebeest leave a strong scent along their trail. This smell allows wildebeest that become separated from the group to get back on track.

Wildebeest have other navigation tools, too. Some of them may have been learned from taking this difficult journey every

Thomson's gazelles feed on the bottom blades of grass that are left over after wildebeest eat.

year. Yet, they also have a remarkable ability: They know where the rain is. Wildebeest can sense rain more than 30 miles (50 km) away. They then travel to the rain-soaked land in time to greet the fresh green shoots of life. Scientists suspect that they use the sound of thunder, the smell of rain, or the sight of dark clouds to guide them.

In addition to weather signals, the millions of wildebeest and other grazers depend on one another to get their food. Although they graze together, each species prefers a different part of the grass. Zebra feed on the tall, tough grasses. Wildebeest follow, munching on the softer shoots exposed by zebra. The smaller Thomson's gazelles eat the bottom blades of grass that are left after the wildebeest feed. These animals also give back to the grassland. The large amounts of dung and urine they leave behind are full of nutrients, which keep the grasses lush and green. Other creatures help these traveling landscapers: Elephants and African buffaloes—which sometimes tag along for short segments of this great migration—clear the path by eating the coarsest, tallest grasses.

DANGER AT EVERY STEP

All migrations are dangerous, but the herds traversing the Serengeti don't seem to get a break. Many fall prey to lions, hyenas, cheetahs, and wild dogs. These predators do not migrate with the herds, but they are almost always around. River crossings can be bloody scenes of death. Driven to reach grassy plains on the other side, thousands of wildebeest will cross powerful rivers, sometimes as many as 20 times in a year. Some will choose difficult crossing sites, or be forced into them to avoid predators or tourist vehicles. They can plunge to their deaths over muddy cliffs. Others will meet the jaws of waiting crocodiles in the river. Many calves will lose their mothers in the chaos of the crossing.

UNDERWATER MARCH OF THE SPINY LOBSTER

Not all walking migrations happen on land. Spiny lobsters live off the Bimini Islands in the Bahamas. They migrate in the ocean, but not by swimming. Instead they walk, single file, on the ocean floor.

Their march begins in the fall with the first storms of the season. Until then, the lobsters spend most daylight hours tucked within the crevices of coral reefs. They come out only at night to feed. The storms seem to signal to the lobsters that their shallow-water homes are no longer safe. They band together and leave for deeper waters, traveling in single file, each lobster touching the tail of the lobster in front of it. For several days, they perform an impressive "follow-the leader" spectacle. They march as much as 30 miles (48 km) nonstop on the ocean floor. Despite currents and an uneven seafloor, the lobsters usually march in straight lines. If a potential predator approaches, they form a circle with their menacing claws facing outward.

Finally, the lobsters arrive at their deep-water destination. In winter, it's warmer here than in shallow water. The warm water seems to help lobster eggs grow faster, and the deeper water keeps the lobsters safer from storms. During the spring and early summer, the lobsters will return to their coral reef. This time there is far less fanfare; the lobsters travel separately at different times.

Spiny lobsters also have extraordinary navigational skills. Like many other animals, they appear to have a built-in magnetic compass. That is, they can tell which direction they are headed. But spiny lobsters also have an

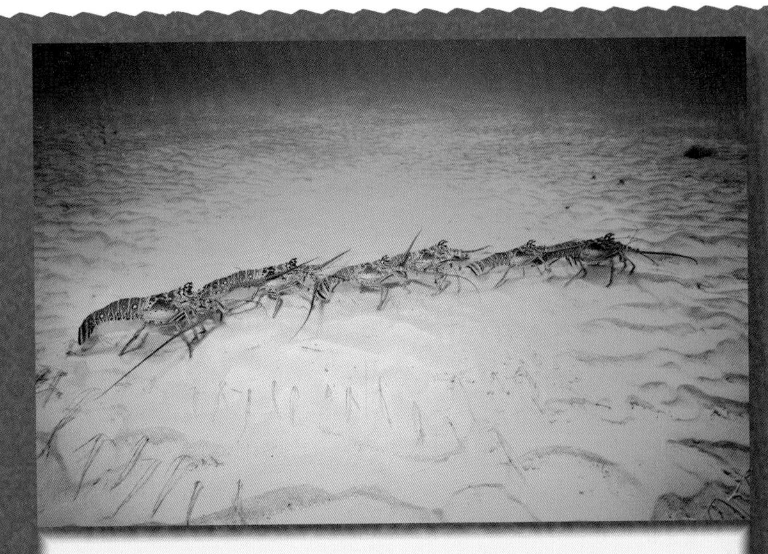

Spiny lobsters migrate together in a single file on the floor of the Atlantic Ocean.

inner sense of exactly where they are on the planet. No other invertebrates (animals without a backbone, such as insects, worms, crabs, and clams) are known to have this talent.

Researchers tested spiny lobsters by moving them as far as 23 miles (37 km) away from their homes. Along the way, they did everything they could to disorient the lobsters. They transported them in swinging, covered containers on circular routes in trucks. They stuck magnets on the containers and covered the lobster's eyes. Still, once the lobsters arrived, they started moving toward home. It seems they can sense Earth's magnetic field. When the researchers created fake fields around them that were only a bit different from the real ones, the lobsters would change their direction in response to the fake fields.

On their own, they will be easy prey for lions and hyenas on the other side.

Yet, perhaps the biggest killer of wildebeest is starvation. Wildebeest are so dependent on grass and water to survive that if a drought strikes, or if barriers such as fences prevent them from reaching greener pastures, they will die.

In an average year, about 250,000 wildebeest die. Those who die are typically the sick, the lame, the old, and the very young. Even so, the herds remain strong. That's because 500,000 new calves join the adults each year. Because they all are born within a few weeks of one another, most calves will escape death by predators, who are simply too overwhelmed and too full to eat them all.

THE LONGEST LAND MIGRATION

While wildebeest are members of the most massive mammal migration, their distant cousins to the far north receive honors for the longest migration of any land mammal. Unlike in the holiday tales, reindeer (aka caribou) can't fly, but they may wish they could. Instead, they walk as many as 3,700 miles (6,000 km). They walk across northern spruce forests and mountain ranges, to the treeless Arctic coast and back again. Reindeer (as they are called in Europe and Asia) or caribou (as they are called in North America) are the thick-furred deer of the north. Both males and females have antlers, which can span 4 feet (1.2 meters).

All caribou belong to the same species (*Rangifer tarandus*), but they live in several separate herds in the Arctic Circle. The largest herds are the Western Arctic herd in northwest Alaska, the George River herd in northern Quebec, and the Taimyr Peninsula herd in Siberia. These herds include at least 500,000 animals each. In the United States, two herds totaling 140,000 caribou (the Porcupine and the Central Arctic herds) travel

Caribou—like these in the Alaskan tundra—take roundabout routes to get to their destinations. Predators, barriers, weather, and other conditions may force them to change course.

within Alaska's Arctic National Wildlife Refuge. This is one of the most remote protected areas in the United States.

The winter and summer ranges of the caribou are 120 miles to 500 miles (200 km to 800 km) apart. The migration distances are much longer, however. Caribou take roundabout routes to get to their destinations. Researchers put radio satellite collars on 70 caribou in northern Quebec. This allowed them to follow each animal's meandering movements. They found that predators, terrain, man-made barriers (such as fences), food sources, and weather may force caribou to change course.

On a sunny winter day in northern Alaska, a 2-foot layer of crusted snow covers the wind-swept ground and the temperature is –15 degrees Fahrenheit (–26 Celsius). Small herds of caribou wander. They stop, paw at the ground, and make little craters with their broad hooves. Then they sniff deeply for **lichens**. It's hardly the moisture-rich green grass that wildebeest feed on in the Serengeti, but lichens are one of the few things that can tolerate the harsh climate. Caribou may spend as many as eight months of each year wandering in small bands, looking for lichens buried under the snow. During the day, they may travel through snowstorms with 50-mile-per-hour (80 km/hr) winds. At night, when temperatures drop to –30 degrees Fahrenheit (–34 Celsius), they may rest in the center of a frozen lake. This is a safer place to watch for potential predators.

A PATH THROUGH ICE AND MOSQUITOES

In April, the weather begins to shift, and so do the caribou. The days grow longer. The caribou begin to move north, toward their birthplace. They leave the scattered spruce forests and cross mountains, heading for the treeless coastal plains. Pregnant females with heavy bellies lead the way. The males may hang back awhile and take shelter in the last of the small, gnarly trees.

Along the way, they meet wolves. Several times, wolf packs attack, taking the slower, weaker animals as their meals. The caribou also must swim across rivers, some with huge ice chunks. Wolves and grizzly bears wait on the other side for those too exhausted to escape them, or for young that have lost their mothers in the crossing.

Small groups of caribou meet along ancient northbound trails, which have been used by generations of caribou. As they travel together, the growing caravan of caribou looks like a black river, with streams rushing in from the sides, flowing through the snowy vastness. When caribou walk, the tendons in their feet slip over bone, making a clicking sound. Multiply one click by four legs and then by more than 100,000 animals, and it sounds like a concert of a million chattering teeth.

By May, the snow is melting. In June, the caribou reach their destination, the tundra of the Arctic coast. The word *tundra* comes from the Finnish word *tunturia*, meaning "barren land." In the winter, the tundra is an icy desert, but in the summer, the tundra is a place of life. Instead of searching for lichens, the caribou feast on grassy plants and mushrooms. They also are safe from wolves. Because the ground is permanently frozen on the tundra, wolves can't make dens for their pups. With food and safety, thousands of caribou give birth. Caribou milk is the richest of all land mammals, and the calves grow quickly. Like the wildebeest, caribou calves are able to run when they are only a few days old.

Though they have plenty of food and few, if any, predators, the caribou face a new hardship: insects. Mosquitoes and biting flies swarm in the damp Arctic summer. The coat of a caribou can appear black, because it is covered in insects. Caribou do what they can to ward off these pests: They stand in thick huddles; they shake and quiver their skin. Still, they may lose up to a quart of blood every week to mosquitoes. This can weaken even a large animal. Caribou also lose precious feeding time while they try to avoid being bitten.

By fall, the urge to return south starts to sweep through the herd. Along the way, they cross rivers, feed as much as they can, and mate. By October, they break up into smaller groups. They will wander again, traveling many miles, in search of lichens under the snow, until they return to the sunny Arctic coast next summer.

TAMING A WANDERER

Caribou are incredibly well equipped for their extreme Arctic journey. Their wooly undercoat has three-inch long outer hairs in the winter. The hairs are hollow, which traps air and insulates the caribou from the cold. The hollow hairs also help caribou float, making them good swimmers. A caribou has an excellent sense of smell. It can sniff out predators, as well as snow-covered lichens.

Caribou hooves change from winter to summer. In the winter, a caribou's footpads grow hard, and a horny edge grows around the outside of each hoof, like a snowshoe. This gives the caribou a larger surface on which to walk. The sharp rim of the hoof can grip slippery ice and dig through crusted snow for lichens. In the summer, the footpads turn spongy. This gives better traction on the soft wet tundra.

The features that make these deer of the north such excellent Arctic survivors also make them useful to people. Arctic cultures in North America and Europe have hunted caribou for thousands of years. They ate the caribou meat and used the hides for clothing. As long as 5,000 years ago, Arctic people began herding reindeer, as they call them, and it's a tradition that continues today. In fact, the Sámi people in Norway, Sweden, and Finland

A CARPET OF CRABS

The migration of the red crab may not win any distance awards, but for sheer numbers—and color—it's one of the more impressive migration spectacles. From the end of October to the beginning of December, visitors to Christmas Island in the Indian Ocean can witness the migration of up to 100 million red crabs.

These brightly colored land crabs march from their forest burrows to the shore. The mass of crabs looks like a huge, moving red carpet. After reaching their coastal destination, the crabs mate. Males dig burrows for the females. The females stay in these shelters for about 12 days, waiting for their eggs to develop. Eventually, the females collectively release billions of fertilized eggs into the ocean. About five weeks later, young crabs will return to the island to follow in their parents' footsteps.

Red crabs make a spectacle when marching to sea off Christmas Island.

A wooly undercoat keeps a caribou well prepared for its Arctic journey. Also, its excellent sense of smell allows it to sniff out snow-covered lichens as well as predators.

and the Nenet and Chukchi people in Russia often are known as "reindeer people." They migrate with the herds, tending them along the way. This ensures a steady source of food and clothing for themselves.

Today, reindeer herds may be guided to different pastures to graze, and so do not migrate as far as they used to. Some reindeer were even tamed enough to be milked and to pull sleds. Reindeer are still herded in some regions for their meat, hides, and antlers.

Tamed reindeer look a bit different from wild reindeer. They have shorter legs. Just one or two wild caribou in a domesticated reindeer herd will make the whole group somewhat restless. It's not certain if they, too, feel the need to migrate.

4

Sharp-Shooters: Salmon and Sea Turtles that Can Find Home

MIGRATION USUALLY INVOLVES regular travel between different places where animals feed, reproduce, and raise their young. Some migrants are flexible about where these places can be located. One example of this are redwings. These birds spend the summer in Russia and northern Europe, yet they may winter in different areas each year. Researchers studying the leg bands on redwings have discovered that the same birds have been found in Britain one year and Greece the next year. The routes and feeding grounds of African wildebeest also vary from year to year, depending on the rains and where the grass grows best. Similarly, fish and whales may stop to feed in a range of cold-water areas, wherever food is abundant.

Other migrating animals are much more particular. They return to specific places, even after thousands of miles of travel. Instead of just returning to a country, or even a neighborhood, they return to the same spot every year. This is called homing behavior. It requires precise navigational skills.

Homing pigeons are a tame version of the rock dove. They were bred for their ability to return to specific locations. They are so precise that for hundreds of years, and even during World War II, they were used to send important messages. Each message was put on a tiny piece of paper, which was tied to the bird's foot.

Other wild birds and animals also have remarkable homing abilities. Bats can return to their homes when they are captured and released 250 miles (400 km) away. Albatrosses are large seabirds. They travel out to sea to feed for weeks at a time before returning to their nests on remote, tiny islands. They can travel over the open ocean for up to 5,000 miles (8,000 km) to collect food. When they are ready to return home they make a straight-line flight of 600 miles (1,000 km) from the ocean to their nests. It is still a mystery how they locate their homes so accurately.

Salmon and sea turtles also have sharp homing skills. The migration of salmon spans freshwater and seawater. Sea turtle migrations also span two worlds: land and ocean. The remarkable thing about both of these migrations is that after years and miles of travel, these animals return to a place they have been only once before—when they were a few days, or even just hours, old.

SALMON: FROM RIVER EGG TO OCEAN FISH

Most salmon begin their life in eggs that are tucked under gravel at the bottom of a cool stream. Just after birth, the salmon are hidden for the moment from hungry birds, raccoons, and other fish. Later, however, these fish will complete a dangerous and precise roundtrip migration from their cool freshwater stream to the massive salty ocean and back again, changing their size and color several times along the way.

There are several species of salmon. Salmon that live in the Pacific Ocean include sockeye, chum, pink, coho, Chinook, and steelhead. One salmon species—the Atlantic salmon—lives in the Atlantic Ocean. Pink salmon are the smallest and generally travel shorter distances. Chinook (also called king) salmon are

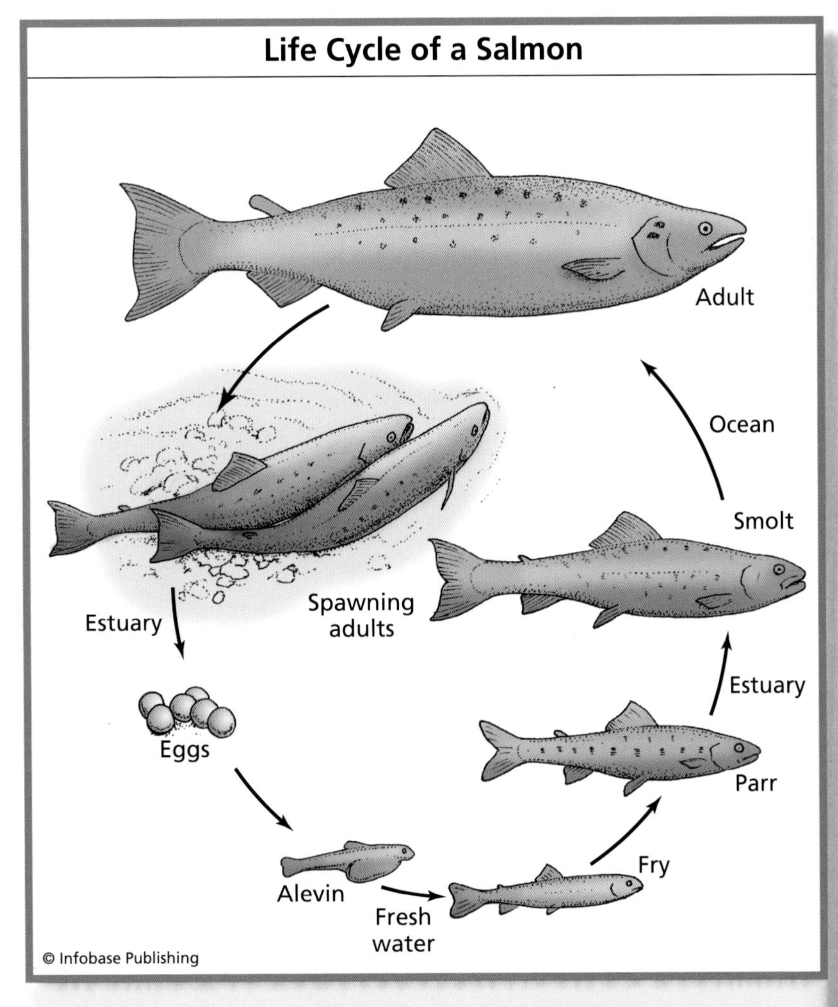

At different stages in a salmon's life, it will live in freshwater, estuaries, and salt water. It will also change in size and color several times along the way.

the largest. They weigh 20 to 60 pounds (9 to 27 kg) and can grow to 58 inches (147 cm) long. Each species differs in the timing and length of its migrations, but they all share a strong drive to return home.

Salmon eggs hatch a month or two after they are laid. This first stage of a salmon's life is called an alevin (pronounced AL-ih-vin). Alevin don't look much like adult salmon. They are pale needles with bright orange potbellies. The orange potbelly is the yolk sac from the egg. It continues to nourish them after they hatch. This way, the alevin can stay protected under the gravel until they are larger.

After about three months of feeding on their yolk sacs, the baby salmon push out of the gravel. Their bodies have changed; they now look more like real fish. At this stage, they are called fry. Depending on the species of salmon, fry will spend only a few months or up to three years living and feeding in streams and lakes. Then, their big journey begins, and the salmon's body changes again. As a young salmon makes its way downstream toward the ocean, it turns silver. These silver-scaled salmon are called smolts.

Smolts may take only a few days or several months before they travel down the stream to the estuary, the place where a river meets the ocean. They spend some time in the estuary feeding and adjusting to the salt water. Once salmon enter the ocean, their traveling is not done. Salmon can spend from one to seven years swimming thousands of miles in broad circles through the ocean.

The long journey to the ocean is worth it. Bountiful ocean eating turns the small smolts, which weigh just a few ounces, into full-size adult salmon. In the ocean, salmon will feed on plankton, squid, small fish, and krill. The pink color of the krill turns salmon flesh bright pink.

THE SMELL OF A STREAM

One to several years after it left its birth stream, a salmon will begin the journey home. From the ocean, salmon gather in large groups—called salmon runs—to swim up rivers, against fierce currents, through rapids, over logs, even up waterfalls. The journey is like trying to walk up a downward escalator. Their determination and strength is amazing. They can wiggle their way through shallow streambeds and leap over obstacles up to 10 feet (3 m) high. Amazingly, all of this is done without eating. Salmon traveling upstream will live off stored fat and protein. Also, salmon lose the slimy coating that protects their scales. Their skin becomes leathery. Salmon also will change colors again, becoming vibrant red or green. This may attract mates. The males grow fangs and hooked noses, which they use in battles with other males over mates.

They may continue this upstream movement for as many as 2,000 miles (3,300 km), through large rivers, winding streams, and narrow creeks, to the place where they once started life as eggs buried in gravel. How do they know where it is? They have been there only once, as many as seven years ago.

Though salmon navigation is still somewhat of a mystery, researchers know some of the tools they use to find their way. To get from the ocean to the start of the correct river, salmon use patterns in the ocean currents, temperature, and even the salinity (saltiness) of the water. Like other migrating animals, salmon also appear to use the sun, stars (imagine a star-gazing fish), and Earth's magnetic field to find their way to the river. These all are cues they would have paid attention to years before, when they left the river and entered the ocean.

Once they are in the river that leads back to their home stream, salmon use their sense of smell to navigate. When salmon leave their home stream, they memorize its odor. The

On its upstream journey back to where it was buried under gravel as an egg, a salmon will face fierce currents and predators.

chemicals in the soil, plants, and insects in a stream have a scent that the salmon recognize and follow. This would be like people sniffing their way to their favorite restaurants from 1,000 miles away.

This understanding of salmon's sniffing ability comes from some interesting experiments. In one study, researchers raised baby salmon in fish tanks. As the fish were turning into smolts, the researchers exposed some of the salmon to a small amount of a smelly chemical not normally found in nature. They marked those fish so they could recognize them again and then released them. Eighteen months later, during spawning season, the researchers put small amounts of that same chemical into a few streams. Then they kept track of which fish came up these streams, as well as other streams. The fish they caught in the chemical-spiked streams were those that had been exposed to the chemical. They swam up streams they had never been to before, just because of a familiar smell. Fish that had not been exposed to these chemicals did not respond to them. This means that when salmon are changing into smolts, they pick up key information about their surroundings: They memorize the smell of home.

In another experiment, scientists plugged salmon's noses. They caught fish swimming upstream, just after they passed a fork in the river. Some of the fish had gone up the east fork and some up the west fork. They caught the fish and then plugged the noses of half the fish with cotton wool. Then they released the fish downstream of the fork, so the fish would have to choose which way to go again. The fish without nose plugs went up the same fork as they did the first time, but the fish with plugged noses didn't seem to know where to go. They randomly chose the east fork or the west fork.

When wild migrating salmon finally reach their birth stream, the female uses her tail to make a gravel hollow where she will lay eggs and the male will fertilize them. Both parents will guard the eggs for a few days. Steelhead and Atlantic salmon will then return to the ocean. An Atlantic salmon may repeat this migration up to seven times in its life. For most salmon species, however, this river-to-ocean roundtrip happens once in a lifetime. Torn up and worn out from their journey, the salmon die in their birth streams.

MYSTERIOUS MIGRATING EELS

The Sargasso Sea lies hundreds of miles off the Atlantic coast of Florida. With warm, deep blue waters and a floating meadow of green seaweed, this may be one of the oddest places on Earth. It has been called the "Sea of Lost Ships," and it overlaps with the infamous Bermuda Triangle, a legendary site of boat and airplane disappearances. Here, two species of eel (the American eel, *Anguilla rostrata,* and the European eel, *Anguilla anguilla*) begin a migration that mirrors the route of salmon. Eels start in saltwater, migrate up freshwater streams, and then return to the saltwater to mate. Like salmon, they go through changes along the way. The eels do not seem to share the salmon's ability to return home. They are much more mysterious.

Newly hatched eels look like transparent ribbons. Following ocean currents, the young eels arrive along the coasts of eastern North America and Europe. During the trip, they change form into something more eel-like and are called glass eels. When they reach the coasts, they migrate into semi-salty waters at the mouths of rivers. Here, they change color and grow. Some eels will remain here. Others, especially females, work their way farther upstream into fresh water. Sometimes they swim several hundred miles, ending in small creeks.

SEA TURTLES RACE TO THE OCEAN

Sea turtles spend most of their life in the water, although they must come to the surface to breathe. The smallest species of sea turtle is the Kemp's Ridley, which can weigh 100 pounds (45 kg) and is more than 2 feet (0.6 m) long. The largest is the leatherback turtle, which can weigh more than 2,000 pounds (900 kg).

Like salmon, the eels swim hundreds of miles upstream, but they have some extra tricks. Their slimy skin is covered with scales that allow them to almost breathe on wet land. On dewy or rainy nights, eels can wiggle their way over wet grass or through wet sand for many miles. Some dams have been covered with Astroturf to make it easier for the eels to climb, and fish ladders have been installed in several rivers to aid their migration. Bodies of eels may pile up by the thousands, climbing over each other to surmount barriers as they slither upstream.

As they grow in their new freshwater homes, they become golden and are called yellow eels. These adult eels may stay in rivers and ponds for up to 30 years, growing up to 5 feet (1.5 m) long. They are active mostly at night, and hide during the day. One summer, an unknown cue will send some eels back downstream, toward the ocean. Along the way they change form once more. Now they are silver eels, with large eyes for seeing in dim ocean water. The females' digestive tracts dissolve, making room for eggs. The eels rely on stored energy to make their final journey, which may be as long as 3,000 miles (4,800 km).

Some silver eels have been tracked heading toward the Sargasso Sea, but none have been found there. It remains a mystery where the adult eels gather. Only their transparent offspring provide a clue as they begin their travels from the Sargasso Sea.

The loggerhead turtle is a migrating sea turtle. It typically takes 5 to 10 years for it to migrate from the shores of eastern Florida, around the Sargasso Sea, and back.

Other migrating sea turtles include the green, the hawksbill, and the loggerhead. The timing and route of each species is different, but they all follow perilous migrations that take them away from the beaches where they are born and then back again.

Like salmon, sea turtles begin their life in eggs. The mothers bury the eggs in the sand along a beach. After as much as a week of hatching and digging their way out of the nest, sea turtles make the first leg of their amazing migration at night. At this moment, the ability to navigate determines a sea turtle's survival. Baby sea turtles are small enough to fit in the palm of a person's hand. They must quickly travel from the beach to the ocean before crabs, raccoons, or other predators on shore snatch them up. How do they know which direction to go?

Sea turtles appear to use one rule: Go to the lightest place on the horizon. Because ocean water reflects more light than land, this rule sends them toward the ocean. However, this navigation trick can fail them. It's not uncommon to see lights on shore on vacation beaches that are lined with hotels. Just one bright light on shore can cause a wrong turn and death for baby sea turtles.

These baby green turtles are heading toward the surf at the Karpas on the island of Cyprus. Cyprus is the third most important place (after Greece and Turkey) for the reproduction of green turtles who come annually by the hundreds between the end of May and the beginning of August to lay eggs.

After reaching the ocean, baby sea turtles will head into oncoming waves to guide them deeper into the ocean. They spend a few days swimming quickly toward deeper waters to avoid being eaten by fish and seabirds. What happens next is a mystery that biologists are starting to uncover. Scientists used to refer to the first few years of a green sea turtle's life as "the lost years." They did not know where the turtles went after they left their home beaches as **hatchlings** and before they showed up in shallow waters, then the size of dinner plates. Recently, biologists traced the paths of some green sea turtles. They used the chemistry of the turtles' shells, which revealed where the turtles were feeding. The turtles were in the open ocean, living among drifting clumps of seaweed and feeding on tiny ocean animals, like plankton, and jellyfish. Young sea turtles may journey through the ocean like this for many years, growing larger. Young loggerheads are born in Florida. They will take 5 to 10 years to complete an 8,000-mile (12,900-km) circuit around the North Atlantic Ocean. Some may make this circular journey repeatedly.

After swimming in the open ocean for up to 25 years, a sea turtle works its way toward shallower waters. Here, it spends the next phase of its life feeding on coastal seaweed and sea grasses. Some species make seasonal north-south migrations along the Atlantic coast to feed. Others, such as the leatherback turtle, continue to wander great distances across the open oceans. When a turtle is ready to reproduce—usually at 25 to 35 years old, but some species aren't ready until 50 years old—it begins a different migration.

BACK TO THE BEACH

To reproduce, sea turtles migrate back to where they were born. In some cases, they must travel long distances. For example, green sea turtles spend most of their time feeding along the coast of Brazil. To return to their birthplaces, they must migrate more than 1,400 miles (2,000 km) to Ascension Island, a speck of an island in the middle of the Atlantic Ocean.

THE LUCKY FEW

Surviving migration is a numbers game. Animals such as salmon and sea turtles overproduce eggs. This ensures that some offspring survive to adulthood. One female salmon will lay thousands of eggs. Chinook, the largest salmon species, can lay up to 8,000. A female sea turtle will lay between 70 to 190 eggs in each sandy nest, depending on the species. Recent studies suggest that some females of some species will visit more than one nesting beach in a season.

With the natural dangers and human-related threats facing salmon and sea turtles today, the numbers of these animals are dwindling. Several populations of salmon, and all sea turtle species, are endangered or threatened. This means that their numbers are so low that the United States government has laws to protect them. Atlantic salmon used to spawn in every river in the Northeastern United States. Now, they are only found in small numbers in Maine. Scientists estimate that out of thousands of Pacific salmon eggs, less than 10 will grow old enough to spawn. The others will be eaten by predators, get caught by fishermen, get stopped by dams along the river, die of disease, suffocate in polluted waters, or not find enough food to fuel their journey back to the spawning grounds. Only 1 out of every 10,000 baby sea turtles will become an adult that returns to its home beach to mate. The others will be eaten (especially if they are disoriented by beach lights), get caught in fishing lines or nets, or choke on plastic floating in the ocean that they mistake for jellyfish.

How do migrating sea turtles find "home" when they haven't seen it since they were less than one day old? Magnets appear to be an important part of the answer. Like birds and other migratory animals, sea turtles can sense Earth's magnetic field. They have an internal compass or sense of direction. More than that, sea turtles appear to have a magnetic map. They can use information about Earth's magnetic field to "figure out" where they are on Earth. Researchers discovered this "map" by testing the direction in which sea turtles swam in tanks. The researchers created an artificial magnetic field that looked like different parts of the turtles' migratory route. The turtles used the information from the magnetic field to swim the correct way. This magnetic

A newborn leatherback sea turtle digs its way out of the sand pit where its mother buried it as an egg. It will now start its journey toward the open ocean.

sensing skill explains how turtles find their home beaches with pinpoint accuracy.

Males and females both make the trip to breeding waters. After mating there, the males will return to the feeding areas. The females stay and make eggs. They fertilize the eggs with sperm from the males.

At high tide about four weeks after breeding, a female green sea turtle swims to the shore at night. Weighing as much as 800 pounds (363 kg), she uses her front flippers to struggle up the sandy ground. This is the first time in many years she has had to move her weight without the support of the water. In the dark, she digs a pit in the sand. With her rear flippers, she carves a burrow in the pit about 3 feet (0.9 m) deep. At this depth, temperature and moisture levels don't change much. After laying more than 100 eggs, she covers them with sand. Within a breeding season, a female green sea turtle might make between one and seven nests. When she's finished, she heads back to the ocean. She will return to this site many times in her life, but rarely every year. Between trips, she will spend several years out in the ocean and swim several thousand miles.

When baby male turtles hatch and rush toward the water, it will be the first and last time they touch land. Surviving baby females will return many years later to repeat their mother's journey.

5

One-Ways, Relays, and Castaways: Animals that Migrate Their Own Way

MOST ANIMAL MIGRATIONS are round-trip journeys made once or many times. The same animal travels between summer and winter homes, or between feeding and breeding areas, each year or every few years. But migration is as varied as the animals that do it. Some animals follow very different paths than others.

Some animals travel only in one direction, never to return to the starting point. One-way migration is called emigration. Animals emigrate because their current home does not meet all of their needs. They must start life in a new home, usually with more or better food. Animals that emigrate include some birds, small mammals (such as lemmings), and insects, including grasshoppers.

Sometimes a roundtrip is completed, but not by one animal. Instead, the animals travel in a relay. Monarch butterflies migrate huge distances between summer and wintering grounds, and they do it by breaking up the trip into several legs. This way, young butterflies, their parents, their grandparents, and even their great-grandparents take part. In this case, the animals will return to a specific "home" they have never actually been to before.

Other animals and insects will hitch a ride to an unknown destination. Small creatures rely on water, air, or other animals to take them places. When they reach a potential new home, they simply jump off.

ONE-WAY WAVES OF LEMMINGS

Lemmings look like large mice, but they are furrier and have short tails. There are many odd tales about how these creatures

There are many myths about lemmings that have stemmed from their unusual migration habits. Scandinavian lemmings, like this Norway lemming, become frantic due to overpopulation and can walk off cliffs because of their focus on moving forward and migrating elsewhere.

live. In the 1500s, some people thought lemmings fell from the sky during storms and then died off when grasses grew tall in the spring. Even today, some people believe lemmings choose to commit suicide by jumping off cliffs. Why did people come up with such strange explanations of lemming behavior? Perhaps because lemmings make an unusual sort of migration.

There are many different species of lemmings. Most live in the far north. They live in North America, Europe, and Asia, in cold forests and the tundra. They feed on plant leaves, roots, and tree bark. When lemmings are not racing over grass, they live in tunnels under the ground or in the snow.

Some lemmings migrate short distances seasonally. In the winter, they live on mountain slopes. There, they feed on plant roots. In the summer, they live in lower, wetter areas. Every three to four years, some types of lemmings have population explosions. Suddenly there are many more lemmings in the same place. When this happens to the brown lemming, which lives in North America, some lemmings go elsewhere. They will travel separately and in different directions. But the Scandinavian lemming does something dramatic. Overpopulation triggers a migration reaction. The lemmings start a frantic and single-minded movement. They are often so focused on moving forward that they can plunge off cliffs. They also move in straight lines, which means lemmings may walk right into houses and boats, instead of around them. The lemmings seem to be searching for higher ground, which is their preferred place to feed.

Many lemmings die from starvation or predators during the migration. For the few that make it to new homes, the flight is worth it. Lemmings typically live less than two years, so they have little time to reproduce. Leaving an overcrowded situation gives lemmings a chance to find a food-rich home. When they get enough to eat, they can have their own young.

SWARMS OF LOCUSTS

High in the sky, it looks like a menacing rain cloud is approaching—it's a dark cloud, more than a mile high. Yet, this cloud does not bring rain. Instead, it follows rain. The cloud is broader than all of New York City and contains billions of flying insects called locusts. In just minutes, they can devour every plant in sight. Even a small swarm of locusts can eat as much food as 2,500 people.

There are several species of locusts. They all migrate, but the desert locust is infamous for the devastation it causes to agriculture and the plants on which people depend. Most of the time,

A swarm of locusts flies over the Okavango Delta in Botswana, Africa.

desert locusts live only in certain deserts in central Africa and the Middle East, where they hop around like grasshoppers. But under the right conditions, things change. When the rains are especially long and heavy, the locusts begin to breed more often. They lay many more eggs than usual. The locust population grows.

When the locusts become overcrowded, they change the way they act and how they look. They start hopping in groups. Sometimes they hop as far as 15 miles (25 km). They change from being light green to brightly colored, with dark markings on their bodies. They also grow wings. These changes are in response to the crowded conditions. Researchers who repeatedly touched the back legs of locusts found that it stimulated them to change from hopping locusts to flying ones.

Once locusts have the power of flight, they travel out of the desert. They seem to fly with the wind and toward rain, which

Locusts breed more when rains are long and heavy. They grow wings when conditions become very crowded. They also become brightly colored with dark markings on their bodies. Desert locusts, like this one, cause devastation to agriculture and plants because of their eating.

means more food. A swarm can travel 120 miles (200 km) a day and continue for many days. One traveling swarm flew a record-breaking 2,800 miles (4,500 km).

As rainy conditions continue, desert locusts keep on breeding and laying eggs. The new locusts will also swarm. This lifestyle can last over several generations. When the food finally runs low and locust numbers drop, they will go back to their lonely on-the-ground grasshopper lives.

A BUTTERFLY RELAY RACE

No other butterfly migrates as far as the monarchs of North America. These wispy, bright-orange fliers are part of an annual migration that covers at least 3,000 miles (4,800 km). Monarch butterflies cannot survive the cold winters found in **temperate** climates. Instead, they spend the winter in roosting spots along the California coast, or in forests in the mountains of Mexico. These are places where the butterflies literally "hang together." They fly in masses to the same winter roosts every year.

A monarch butterfly weighs less than a paperclip and has a 4-inch (10-cm) wingspan. How does it make the long trip? It shares the journey with its relatives. Instead of one butterfly making the whole trip, several generations of butterflies engage in a relay race: After a butterfly dies, one of its offspring continues the journey. One member, though, will take most of the trip. Their unusual way to travel was discovered only over many years by placing tiny stickers on their wings and finding them again just a few or up to thousands of miles away.

Monarch butterflies, like all butterflies, do not spend all their lives with wings. Each monarch begins as a tiny egg on a leaf. After about four days, out comes a caterpillar, which feeds on the leaves of plants. For monarch caterpillars, only one type of plant will do—and that's milkweed. Milkweeds are a group of

Placing stickers on the wings of monarch butterflies helps scientists track their migration patterns.

flowering plants with a white, milk-like sap inside. They grow naturally in North American grasslands. The plant contains poisons, but they don't upset the butterflies. In fact, eating milkweed gives monarch butterflies a sort of "superpower." The monarchs take the poisons into their bodies, which makes them taste awful to predators.

After feasting on milkweeds for about two weeks, the plump caterpillar becomes enveloped in a hard green covering, called a chrysalis, which is dotted with some magical-looking gold spots. Over the next 10 days, the caterpillar transforms into a butterfly.

In the grasslands of the eastern United States, monarch butterflies born in the spring and summer will live for two to six weeks. They feed on flower nectar, mate, and lay eggs. As they do this, they travel a little northward, following the new growth of milkweed plants, which depend on warmer weather to grow. After seven months and four or five generations of monarchs, the butterflies will have traveled from southern states to northern states.

Monarchs born in August and September experience different conditions. The days are shorter and cooler, and the milkweed is a little less nutritious. Now, it is time to go south instead of continuing north like their parents, grandparents, and great-grandparents. This south-bound generation will live very differently from its spring- and summer-born relatives. For one thing, the butterflies will live longer. Eating nectar along the way, these monarchs fly from the Eastern United States or Canada to Mexico. (A smaller population of monarchs that lives west of the Rockies spends the winter in groves of eucalyptus, pine, and cypress trees along the California coast.) Wind currents help the butterflies along this 2,000-mile (3,219-km) journey, but it still takes about two months and some precise navigation.

In the cool mountains of west-central Mexico, monarch butterflies gather. Almost all the monarchs of North America meet

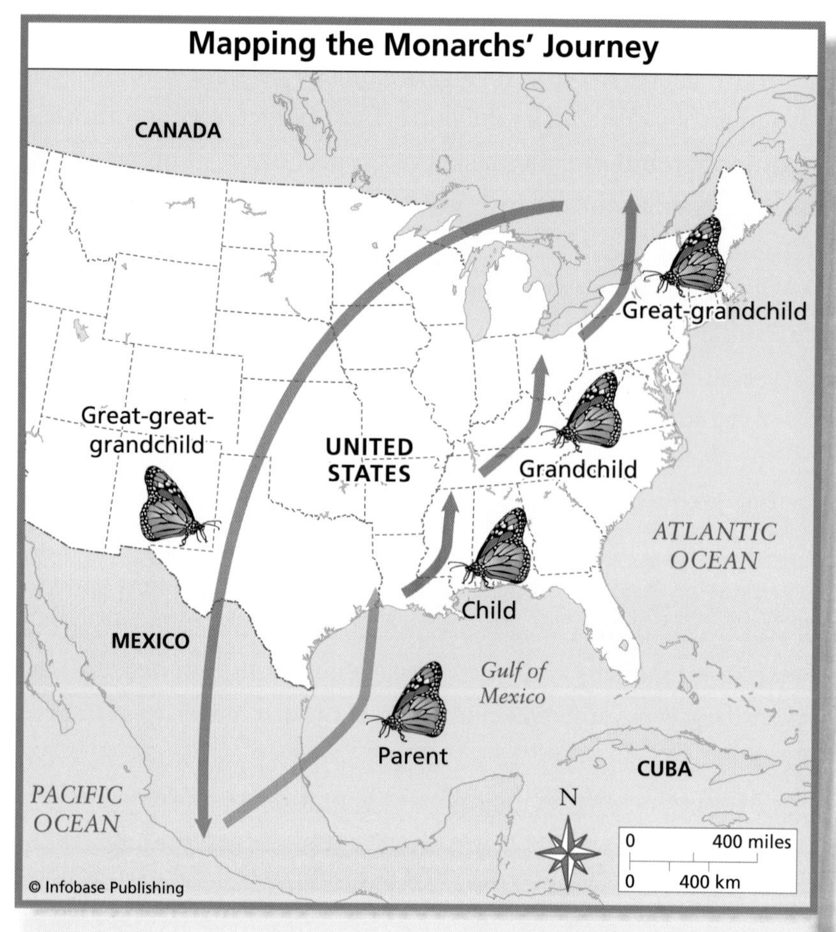

The long trip of the monarch butterfly is shared among several generations.

up in a dozen small forests scattered throughout an area about the size of Delaware. As many as 400 million butterflies come here. These forests include only one type of tree, the oyamel fir. A single tree can be 100 feet (30 m) tall. In the winter, it will be blanketed in butterflies. Unfortunately, oyamel firs also are popular for their wood. People cut them down and sell them. As

In the cool mountain forests of west-central Mexico, monarch butterflies blanket the oyamel fir trees by hanging in a kind of sleep state.

the forests get smaller, so do the numbers of butterflies that can survive the winter.

Monarch butterflies will stay in these cool mountain forests for five or six months. They can live this long because they do very little. They don't eat much. They spend most of the time hanging from the trees in a kind of sleep. Occasionally, when the sun warms them, they will fly off to streams or puddles to drink water, or to flowers for nectar.

In early spring, the monarchs begin part three of their lives. These same butterflies, which traveled so far south and remained in a sleepy state for months, will start mating. Soon after mating, they head north. They only go as far as the southern Gulf States, though they might have started the previous fall in Canada. When they find milkweed plants, the females lay eggs. Exhausted and tattered, having lived longer and traveled farther than generations before them, they die. The caterpillars that hatch from their eggs will start the slow movement northward as butterflies, beginning the cycle again.

FINDING A FOREST FOR THE FIRST TIME

The monarch butterflies that return to Mexico will be the great-great grandchildren of those that went the winter before. How they know where to go when they have never been to Mexico before is one of migration's great mysteries. There are many ideas, but none has been proven. Although a monarch butterfly's brain is not much larger than a grain of sand, the butterflies probably use a combination of navigational tools to find their way. Like birds, they use the sun to guide them. Monarch butterflies use the angle of the sun in the sky, together with an accurate built-in clock, to figure out direction. On cloudy days, monarchs can still use the sun's rays, which are invisible to people, to guide them.

SPECIAL DELIVERY

Many migrating animals take something with them as they move from place to place. What they carry turns out to be crucial to the survival of many other plants and animals. This makes migrants one of nature's most important delivery systems.

Animals that eat fruit often drop the seeds much farther away from where they found the fruit. This spreads the seeds. New fruit trees grow in different places, providing food for other animals. Many migrating birds spread seeds, but other migrating animals do it, too. In Australia, the gray-headed flying fox (which is really a large bat) can transport the seeds of rainforest trees more than 19 miles (30 km) away. These animals migrate as many as 1,243 miles (2,000 km).

(continues)

Picking up pollen from flowers and carrying it to other flowers aids in the development of more plants. The ruby-throated hummingbird performs this action along its migratory route.

(continued)

Traveling animals that feed on the nectar of flowers also perform a service. Each time they visit a flower, they also pick up some dust-like pollen. When they visit the same species of plant again, this pollen fertilizes the egg in the flower, producing a seed. These seeds make more plants, which means more nectar and other foods (fruits, leaves, roots). Along its migratory route, a monarch butterfly or a ruby-throated hummingbird ensures the making of millions of seeds.

Seeds and pollen are not the only life-giving things migrating animals carry. Salmon spend months or years feeding in the ocean. Then they return to their freshwater homes, many miles inland up rivers. Bald eagles, grizzly bears, and other animals rely on salmon as part of their diet. But more than that, salmon are like a traveling bag of fertilizer. A salmon's body carries nutrients from the ocean. When they die after spawning, their bodies break down and releases those nutrients. Plants and small animals in the streams, that support so many other larger animals, would not grow without the living fertilizer of salmon.

Just heading south or southwest would not be enough to get a monarch to its destination. It needs to find precise patches of forest. Like some other migrating animals, monarchs have magnetite in their bodies, so they may be able to sense Earth's magnetic field. Yet, experiments haven't shown that monarchs change direction based on the magnetic field. Monarchs could use landmarks to find their way. Coastlines or chains of mountains may be like paths that the butterflies can follow. Once they get close to the forests, the smell of dead butterflies there from the year before may help them zero in on the right spot. But this idea hasn't been tested. Figuring out exactly how monarch butterflies find their way will take many more careful studies.

HITCHHIKERS AND CASTAWAYS

Many migrating animals use their own power to get where they need to go. Yet, others go wherever their "vehicle" takes them. Without much control over speed or direction, these migrants ride the wind, water currents, or other animals.

Some spiders are very good at taking free rides in the air. Gossamer spiders use the silk they weave to travel to new locations. They seem to travel in order to avoid competition with their neighbors, or to escape danger. The spider climbs to higher ground and stands on its tiptoes with its belly facing upward. It then produces strands of silk that blow in the breeze. It spins the lines longer and longer, until the wind pulls at the silk and lifts the spider into the air. Traveling as high as three miles (4.8 km) into the sky, the spider may go hundreds of miles. It is not uncommon for gossamer spiders to land on islands in the middle of an ocean. No one knows how much control these spiders have over where they land.

Other arachnids, insects, and animals have come up with another solution to travel. They hitch a ride on another animal. The pseudoscorpion is a spider relative. It looks like a tiny scorpion. Some pseudoscorpions will attach themselves to flies, beetles, or mice. They hitch a ride and drop off when they find a better place. Mites also ride on other animals. Flower mites feed on the nectar and pollen of flowers. They travel to new plants with the help of hummingbirds. When a hummingbird is sucking nectar from a flower, a mite will run into the bird's nose in less than a second. At another flower, it runs out again. It decides where to jump off by taking a quick whiff of each flower that the hummingbird is sniffing.

6

Survivors: Moving in a Modern World

MIGRATING ANIMALS ARE real survivors. Along their journeys they face many dangers. Predators eat them. Storms and severe weather can throw them off course. They may run out of food and energy before they reach a destination. Yet, migrants keep doing it because this traveling lifestyle is often necessary to find food, milder weather, mates, or safety for their young.

Still, something that has worked for so long may now be starting to fail. New dangers exist. Forests, meadows, oceans, and rivers are changing. Some have become shopping centers, houses, or fields of corn. Roads and fences block migration paths. Earth's climate is also changing: Spring starts earlier, and the ice near the North and South Poles is melting.

All of these changes may affect any plant or animal, but migrating animals are especially vulnerable because of how they live. Taking lengthy journeys means that migrants are more likely than nonmigrants to cross paths with human activities. On its migratory route, a salmon may pass through forests logged for timber, farmland sprayed with pesticides, dams, bustling cities and towns, and shipping routes. Because of all of this, many migratory animals are already dropping in numbers. Some are in danger of becoming **extinct**.

EASY TARGETS

Hundreds of years ago, the sailors who first explored the world knew a good place to find fast food. Compared with solo animals swimming swiftly in the ocean, huge numbers of lumbering sea turtles on beaches were easy pickings—and so were their eggs. The sailors collected thousands of sea turtle adults and eggs. Whales used to be hunted around the world as well (now regulated hunting is only permitted with regulations in Alaska, Japan, and Iceland, among a few other places.) Hundreds of years ago, they were often hunted for their blubber, which was turned into oil to light lamps. It took many months on the open sea to hunt a whale. Yet, in the mid-1800s, hunters discovered small Mexican lagoons where whales gathered to safely give birth to their young. Herds of whales were quickly killed.

Other migratory animals are easy targets, too. They are found in large numbers in small areas: their breeding or feeding places. They tend to be at those places at the same times each year. Even when migrating animals do not gather in single spots, they can become easy targets when they travel the same routes. Ducks and geese will gather at favorite feeding grounds during their migrations. Once hunters discover the right places and times, the animals can be hunted intensely.

Many people cannot imagine that hunting could harm animals that appear in so many different places and are so abundant. There just seem to be too many of them to matter. Yet, many migratory animals have gone from millions to few or even none, in short amounts of time. Bison, the largest land mammals of North America, used to fill the plains of the central United States. Like the wildebeest of Africa, or the caribou of the north, great herds of the American "buffalo" would migrate throughout the plains each year. In 1800, there may have been as many as 60 million bison. After less than a hundred years of being hunted for food, fur, sport, and even to make leather belts that ran industrial machines, there were less than 300 bison left in the wild. They have since increased in numbers, but not to the levels they once were.

A computer-generated image shows a passenger pigeon, a migratory animal that was hunted to extinction.

Some migratory animals were hunted to extinction. The passenger pigeon was once the most abundant bird in North America. Each year, this large dove-like bird would migrate from eastern and central North America to Mexico and Cuba. They lived in large, social groups. There were so many passenger pigeons that flocks of migrants would take several days to pass one spot. A cloud of billions of birds 1 mile (1.6 km) wide and 300 miles (500 km) long would block the sun. Their numbers made them easy targets. Starting in the early 1800s, passenger pigeons were hunted for food and fun. Less than a hundred years later, they were gone.

Many laws now prevent animals from being hunted to extinction. The Endangered Species Act protects several migratory animals in the United States, including sea turtles. They may not be hunted, harassed, or even held without a special permit.

Other animals are still hunted, but there are limits on the numbers and ages of the animals that can be taken. The idea is to prevent animals from being killed faster than they can reproduce. But sometimes it is hard to know the "magic number" of animals that can be taken without causing a problem. If the number is too high, or if the laws are not followed, the animals will not survive. For example, bluefin tuna migrate across the Atlantic Ocean twice a year. They are caught in many different places along their route. All of this fishing, some of it illegal, is bringing this migrant close to extinction.

OBSTACLE COURSE

Migrating animals face another challenge in today's world. In addition to mountains or rivers they must cross, there are modern barriers. For walkers, this includes fences and roads. In Botswana, a country in southern Africa, more than 500 miles (805 km) of wire fencing cuts across the Okavango Delta, an oasis

HORSESHOE CRAB DOMINOES

What would it matter if one migratory animal goes extinct? If it is just a visitor wherever it goes, then does it make a difference? It turns out that many migrating animals are like the first piece in a line-up of dominoes. If they go down, it affects many other animals.

The horseshoe crab has been around for about 350 million years. Hundreds of thousands of migratory shorebirds, especially the red knot, rely on the migration of the horseshoe crab. Each spring, horseshoe crabs swim up from deeper waters in the Atlantic Ocean to a spawning area near the Delaware Bay. Millions of crabs lay eggs in the wet sand. Some of these eggs are crucial meals for migrating birds.

The connection between the birds and the crabs was not clear until the 1990s. There were fewer crabs and fewer birds gathering on the shore each year. Meanwhile, fishermen were catching horseshoe crabs without any limits. They used them as bait to catch other fish. Since then, laws were passed to protect the horseshoe crab. Yet, recovery is slow and both crab and bird numbers are still low.

Horseshoe crabs' eggs are a key part of the diet of migrating birds.

of water in a huge desert. The fences are meant to keep cattle from getting diseases from wildlife, but many wild animals rely on this water, especially in drought years. Wildebeest migrate in Botswana, though in smaller numbers than in the Serengeti. Thousands of wildebeest have died along this barrier because they could not reach water after hundreds of miles of travel.

A road does not need to be a major highway to stop a migrant in its tracks. Even a small road can be a barrier for a migrating frog. Wood frogs are small singing frogs that live in wooded areas. Each spring, they migrate to ponds or pools. There, they find mates and lay eggs. Then they return to the woods. Wood frogs often must cross roads on their way to and from ponds. Many get run over by cars. In some places where large numbers of frogs cross, people have built tunnels to protect them (and other animals) from this danger. These passages allow frogs, salamanders, snakes, tortoises, and other animals to pass *under* roads instead of over them.

Swimmers face obstacles when migrating, too. Some animals travel through or near shipping lanes, the busy highways of the ocean. There, ships transport materials along coastlines or between continents. Animals may collide with these ships. This is a common cause of death for migrating right whales on the Atlantic coast. Some shipping lanes off Canada and Massachusetts have been moved to avoid collisions with right whales.

Huge nets or fishing lines also can stop ocean migrants. Whales and sea turtles need to come to the surface to breathe. They can get caught in nets or discarded fishing gear. Some fishing lines are several miles long and have hundreds or thousands of baited hooks. Seabirds get caught on these as they try to take the bait on the surface of the water. Sea turtles get caught in the lines or get hooked underwater.

In rivers, dams stop the natural flow of water. Some dams are built to hold water in place for humans to use, or to use the

Roads can be dangerous barriers for traveling animals. This sign warns drivers to look out for the nene, a variety of Hawaiian goose, which is also the Hawaiian state bird.

water to turn machines that make electricity. For salmon, eels, or other fish traveling up or down a river, a dam can mean the end of the trip. Salmon cannot travel up rivers with large dams. They are lost from these rivers completely. Once people discovered the problems that dams create, some unused dams were removed. In some cases, fish ladders were installed to allow fish to travel across dams. A fish ladder is like a staircase made of water pools. Salmon can leap from pool to pool. Some dams have been covered with a textured, grass-like surface to allow eels to "climb" over.

Fliers also must deal with obstacles along their migratory paths. Tall metal towers used for cell phones, pagers, televisions, and radios can get in the way. In the United States alone, there are more than 140,000 towers, and new ones continue to be built. Birds can crash into these towers, especially if they have red lights on them at night.

To a bird that has evolved to fly at night, with nothing but the light of the stars and the moon, any light can be a traffic hazard. Birds have been known to circle around lights or brightly lit buildings until they are exhausted or they collide with the building or post. Power lines also can be low and invisible enough to be in the way, especially to birds with large wingspans like cranes, raptors, and swans. Collisions with power lines are one of the major causes of death of sandhill cranes. Glass windows are also invisible to fast flying birds who may simply see the reflection of sky or trees and fly straight into the glass. To avoid these fatal collisions, some people put stickers on the glass that look like hawks to keep birds away.

ARE WE THERE YET?

In spite of these obstacles, many migrants still arrive at their destinations. But sometimes, when they get there, the place is not what it used to be. Maybe it no longer has the food they need or the safe places to raise their young. To make matters worse, the migrants are tired. They have no food or extra energy, and have little time to find a better place.

More migratory animals are facing this dilemma as their **habitats**, or the land and oceans they depend on, are changing. In some cases, the change may be quite dramatic. A previous destination or critical layover spot becomes unrecognizable. Many forests have been turned into parking lots, with little to offer a migratory bird, frog, or bat. A forest or natural grassland may be converted into a cornfield or cow pasture. Loss of habitat is a main reason that migratory animals start to disappear.

Fish ladders, like this one at the Bonneville Dam in Oregon, are built to help fish travel across dams.

Some habitats are not lost, but they're not what they used to be. A forest may have been cut up into smaller parcels surrounded by farmland and houses. It is harder for birds to live in these forest fragments. They offer less food and are not as safe. Birds are more exposed to cats and other predators.

Changes in the water can affect swimmers. When a forest near a stream is cut down, the water is less shaded. More dirt washes into it. Because salmon need cool, clean water, these streams are no longer good places to spawn. Many rivers have become polluted from chemicals that wash into them. Laws to that prevent water pollution can help make streams, rivers, lakes, and oceans better places for all the animals that live there.

IS IT TIME TO GO?

For migrants, timing is key. They must be in the right place when the right food is available. If they arrive too early or too late, they may starve. Animals tend to use changes in the amount of daylight to cue them when it is time to go. But their food sources—caterpillars, plants, plankton—rely mostly on temperature to grow.

The global climate is changing. Some places in the world are warmer than they used to be. Burning fossil fuels, such as oil and gas, changes the air. The changes cause the air to hold in more heat from the sun, causing **global warming**. This slow but real increase in temperature means all sorts of changes in climate, or long-term weather.

Even a change of a few degrees could throw off the perfect timing needed for migration to work. Pied flycatchers are sleek little black-and-white birds that migrate between Europe and Africa. They are suffering from a climate change mismatch. They arrive in Europe in the spring to breed and feed their chicks. Usually, their arrival is perfectly timed with a plentiful food

In an example of deforestation, this tropical rainforest in Brazil has been partially cut down to grow a soy field. Deforestation makes it hard for animal inhabitants because it means less food and fewer safe places to raise young.

source: newly hatched caterpillars. With warmer weather, spring is starting earlier in northern Europe. More than 2,000 miles away in Africa, the birds do not know that spring has arrived up north. They leave at their usual time. But that is now too late. By the time they arrive, there aren't as many caterpillars. Many chicks starve, because the food source they have come to depend on is not abundant when they are born.

Gray whales also are affected by climate change. Scientists have watched these animals migrate up and down the Pacific coast for years. Now, scientists are noticing that some of the whales are

NEXT STOP: YOUR BACKYARD

After a long flight, a stop at a bush full of berries is a needed feast for migrating birds. These "in-flight meals" are key to making sure the birds can reach their final destination. Butterflies also need energy during their trips: They must find enough flowers with energy-packed nectar, as well as the right plants on which to lay their eggs. The birds, butterflies, frogs, and bats that your yard or parks near your home may have come from just a few miles away, or thousands of miles away. This spot can be a refueling station, or a seasonal home.

Creating habitat for migrating animals can be as simple as planting bushes that make fruits at the right time of year. Migrating birds love the fruits of eastern red cedar. A shrub like Arrowwood viburnum shelters, nests, and makes clusters of tiny blue berries in September, right when birds

(continues)

Asters bloom in the fall and are often covered by monarch butterflies in need of nectar before their journey south.

(continued)

heading south need extra fuel. Bee balm and phlox have nectar-rich flowers that can give butterflies and humming-birds the energy they need to travel. Monarch butterflies heading south will feed on the nectar of asters, small purple, daisy-like flowers. This gives them the fat reserves to make it through the winter.

A small pond in your backyard can give a crucial replenishing drink to migrants. It also can be a breeding destination for frogs. A migration-friendly backyard is free of chemicals, such as pesticides. Pesticides might kill off mosquitoes and biting flies, but they also can poison butterflies, as well as the birds and frogs that eat insects. A better backyard bug repellent is a wooden bat house, which is like a birdhouse but with an entrance hole on the bottom. This can be a summer home for migrating brown bats, each of which can gobble up 600 mosquitoes in an hour.

The areas around houses, schools, and other buildings can have enough food and shelter for migrating animals. If so, migrants that have lost their larger forest or grassland may still find what they need. Many migrating animals will even make someone's yard their summer or winter home. The same animals will return to the same spot each year. Others might just stop by to rest and refuel on their way from a tropical rainforest in South America to the Canadian tundra.

very thin. Their bones are sticking out. The whales also seem to be spending more time in their northern feeding grounds before heading south and are having fewer calves. Because the northern waters are getting warmer, the whale's main food source, krill, is decreasing. Krill live in cold waters. Whales now may have to travel farther and use more energy to get the food they need.

The tundra—a summertime destination for many migrants—is especially sensitive to climate change. Here, the ground is permanently frozen and no trees grow. It does not sound like a great place, but for many migrating animals, it is ideal. In the brief summer months, when the sun's rays warm it up, the tundra explodes into a lush, green, insect-filled, mucky plain. Because few animals live there year-round, visitors have little competition for food, and there are few predators. It is an ideal place for birds like geese, ducks, and shorebirds to lay their eggs and feed. Herds of caribou can chomp on greens. Safe from wolves, they give birth to their calves. Because of global warming, however, some parts of the tundra are defrosting. Trees can now take root in the ground. There is no longer an open plain. Migrating animals that travel thousands of miles to reach the tundra will have to go even farther north.

ANCIENT TRADITIONS, MODERN PACE

It is difficult to know how long yearly migrations have been happening. Some are ancient. Gray whales have swum in the oceans for 30 million years. Giant birds migrated as many as 80 million years ago. Sea turtles have lived in the oceans for about 150 million years. They were around when the dinosaurs became extinct.

Some migrating animals have carried on through ice ages. These were years when forests might have been covered with a mile-high layer of ice. If migrating animals could handle an ice age, why would they have problems with a few new roads, a mall parking lot, or a few degrees of temperature change? One reason is time.

Changes today are happening much faster than before. During an ice age, the temperature changed less than half a degree every 1,000 years. Today, Earth's temperature has increased

1 degree in just 100 years. Pollution, new roads, and loss of wilderness have also dramatically changed habitats.

Why are faster changes more of a challenge for animals? Adapting to change takes time. Some of the details of migration are hard-wired. A sea turtle, for example, may continue to lay eggs on the beach where it was born, even if the beach now has brightly lit hotels that will disorient its babies. Over time, those sea turtles that continue to go to the hotel-filled beach will not reproduce as well. Sea turtles that go to a safer beach, if there is one, will have more babies that survive. These could be the ones to continue the species and change the pattern of migration.

Many migrating animals managed to adapt to slow changes in the past. Sadly, some of these animals cannot survive the rapid changes taking place today. Bluefin tuna are being fished faster than they can reproduce. Caribou may die in many of the places they roam. With heavy coats and no ability to sweat, they are so adapted to cold weather that warmer summers can kill them.

Other animals may adapt to a world shared with humans. Some birds, like the European blackcap, are not migrating as far south as they used to. They are adapting to the warmer winters. Loggerhead sea turtles are adjusting to a changing climate by laying their eggs about 10 days earlier than they did 15 years ago. However, even if some animals can adapt slightly or slowly to a modern world, most will need help to survive.

A HELPING HAND

Help for migrating animals can come in many forms. Migrating animals will benefit from having places where they will not be hunted, face obstacles, or have their habitat destroyed. Protected parks can do this. The Serengeti National Park and Masai Mara National Reserve (connected across Tanzania and Kenya) have allowed the magnificent wildebeest migration to continue.

Animals also may benefit from laws that regulate how many can be hunted. If these laws are created early enough and if they are followed, they can reverse a population decline. Gray whales migrating along the Pacific Coast have made a miraculous recovery since hunting stopped. Of course, any efforts to protect migrating animals must consider that the animals do not care about political boundaries. They may migrate across states, countries, and even continents. Often, no single government can ensure a safe journey, but international agreements can. Canada, the United States, and Mexico have come up with a shared plan

Whooping cranes were taught by humans how to migrate again after they came dangerously close to extinction.

for regulating hunting and protecting the habitats of migrating ducks, geese, and swans.

Other help for migration will come in the form of devices or technology, such as fish ladders to help salmon travel up dammed rivers. A less bright or different-colored light bulb can be a simple solution to stop confusing migrating birds or baby turtles on beaches. To keep sea turtles from getting caught in nets used to catch shrimp, scientists developed "turtle excluder devices." These gated openings allow larger animals like sea turtles and sharks to push out of nets.

Sometimes it is even possible to teach an animal to migrate again. The whooping crane, the tallest bird in North America, was once very close to extinction. It used to live in areas from Canada to Mexico and from Utah all the way to the Atlantic coast. As the human population increased, the whooping crane's habitat disappeared. The cranes were also hunted and their eggs collected. In 1941, only 15 birds were left. Since then, whooping cranes have been raised in captivity. There are close to 300 birds now. The trick to helping these birds was restoring their annual southward migration.

William Lishman and Joe Duff helped the whooping cranes migrate to Florida. They founded a company called Operation Migration. Lishman and Duff relied on a hard-wired behavior called imprinting. A newly hatched chick will trust and follow the first moving object it sees. The men help the baby birds imprint on the aircraft and teach them to fly behind it. In fall 2001, whooping cranes migrated from Wisconsin to a safe wintering site in Florida by following an ultra-light aircraft. In the spring of 2002, these birds returned to Wisconsin on their own. In 2006, a whooping crane chick made its way to Florida with its parents instead of a plane. It was the first whooping crane hatched in the wild to migrate to Florida in more than a century, and it helped prove that people can help animals thrive.

Glossary

amphibian A class of animals that spends part of its time on land and part in the water, such as frogs and salamanders

arctic The region around Earth's North Pole, characterized by very cold temperatures

breeding The act of reproduction of species

breeding ground A place where animals give birth to or hatch their offspring

echolocation The use of sound like sonar and radar by animals (such as whales and bats) to locate objects in the surrounding environment

extinction No longer existing on Earth

global warming An increase in Earth's average surface temperature caused by human activities, such as burning coal, oil, and natural gas

habitats Places where animals live, including the physical conditions (like water and temperature) and the other plants and animals they need to be able to grow and reproduce

hatchling A bird, fish, or reptile (including turtle) that has just hatched from its egg

homing The ability to return to a specific place

krill Tiny shrimp-like creatures that live in the open seas and are a major part of the diet of baleen whales

lichens A crusty or scaly plant-like fungus that typically grows on rocks or trees; it is resistant to cold and dryness and can grow in areas such as Arctic tundra.

magnetic field A detected force that exists around a magnet or electrical field; Earth's magnetic field has north and south poles linked by lines of magnetic force.

magnetite An iron-containing mineral that is magnetic, acting much like a needle in a compass

migratory restlessness A behavior seen in captive migratory animals, especially birds, when they are especially active or restless, trying to move in particular directions at certain times of the year

navigation The process of finding one's way from one place to another

population A group of animals of the same species, living in the same area

predator Any animal that kills and eats another animal

raptors Large birds like hawks, eagles, or falcons that hunt for smaller birds and mice

satellite tag A small device that can be attached to an animal and then relay information on the animal's whereabouts to satellites orbiting Earth

shorebirds Birds with webbed feet typically seen on sandy shorelines and in marshes and bays

spawn To release eggs that will hatch into young, as fish or frogs do

species A group of related organisms with common characteristics that breed with each other

synchronized Occuring at the same time

tundra Areas near the North Pole where there are no trees, the ground is frozen much of the year, and the plants are mostly mosses, lichens, and grass-like plants called sedges

vertical migration Migration in an up-and-down movement, rather than a north-and-south movement

zooplankton Tiny, drifting animals in oceans, rivers, or lakes; they are mostly small crab-like animals and the larvae or young of fish

Bibliography

Anderson, Edward William. *Animals as Navigators*. New York: Van Nostrand Reinhold, 1983.

Baker, Robin. *The Mystery of Migration*. New York: Viking Press, 1981.

Boles, L.C. and K.J. Lohmann. "True navigation and magnetic maps in spiny lobsters." *Nature* 421 (2003):60–63.

Borner, Markus. "The Great Migration," Serengeti, Tanzania National Parks Web Site. Available online. URL: www.serengeti.org/download/Migration.pdf

Boustany, Andre M., Scott F. Davis, Peter Pyle, Scot D. Anderson, Burney J. Le Boeuf, and Barbara A. Block. "Satellite tagging: Expanded niche for white sharks." *Nature* 415 (3 January 2002): 35-36.

Bradshaw, William E. and Christina M. Holzapfel. "Evolutionary Response to Rapid Climate Change." *Science* Vol. 312. no. 5779 (9 June 2006): 1477–1478.

Dalton, Rex. "More Whale Standings Are Linked To Sonar." *Nature* 440 (30 March 2006): 593.

Day, Stephen. "Science: Migrating Birds Use Genetic Maps to Navigate." New Scientist Web Site. Available online. URL: http://www.newscientist.com/article/mg13017654.000-science-migrating-birds-use-genetic-maps-to-navigate-.html

Ellis, D., W. Sladen, W. Lishman, K. Clegg, J. Duff, G. Gee, and J. Lewis. "Motorized migrations: The future or mere fantasy?" *Bioscience* 53 (March 2003): 260–264.

Elphick, Jonathan. *The Atlas of Bird Migration: tracing the great journeys of the world's birds*. Buffalo, N.Y.: Firefly Books, 2007.

Finney, Ben. "A Role for Magnetoreception in Human Navigation?" *Current Anthropology* Vol. 36, No. 3. (June 1995): 500-506.

Gagliardo, A., P. Ioalè, M. Savini, and J. M. Wild. "Having the nerve to home: trigeminal magnetoreceptor versus olfactory mediation of homing in pigeons." *Journal of Experimental Biology* 209 (August 2006): 2888 -2892.

Hansford, Dave. "Alaska Bird Makes Longest Nonstop Flight Ever Measured." National Geographic News Web Site. Available online. URL: http://news.nationalgeographic.com/news/2007/09/070913-longest-flight.html

Hooper, Rowan. "Humpback Whales Boast the Longest Mammal Migration." New Scientist Web Site. Available online. URL: www.newscientist.com/article/dn11544-humpback-whales-boast-the-longest-mammal-migration.html

Jones, Geoffrey P., Serge Planes, and Simon R. Thorrold. "Coral Reef Fish Larvae Settle Close to Home." *Current Biology* 15 (July 2005): 1314–1318.

Kirschvink, Joseph L. "Magnetite Biomineralization and Geomagnetic Sensitivity in Higher Animals: An Update and Recommendations for Future Study." *Bioelectromagnetics* 10 (1989): 239–259.

Lohmann, K.J. "Orientation and Navigation of Sea Turtles," Lohmann Lab, University of North Carolina, Department of Biology Web Site. Available online. URL: http://www.unc.edu/depts/oceanweb/turtles/

Lorenzi, Rossella. "Reindeer Threatened by Warmer Weather." Discovery Channel News Web Site. Available online. URL: http://dsc.discovery.com/news/briefs/20041206/reindeer.html

Lowrey, Peter. "Hunger in their wake: inside the battle against the desert locust," Food and Agriculture Organization of the United Nations Newsroom, October 2004. Available online. URL: http://www.fao.org/newsroom/en/focus/2004/51040/index.html

McNeil Jr., Donald G. "Fly Away Home." *New York Times*. (October 3, 2006)

National Marine Fisheries Service. "Annual Report to Congress: 1999–2000 Administration of the Marine Mammal Protection Act of 1972," National Oceanic and Atmospheric Administration, National Marine Fisheries Service Web Site. (2000) Available online. URL: http://www.nmfs.noaa.gov/prot_res/readingrm/MMPAannual/1999_2000_mmparep.pdf

Roach, John. "Albatrosses Fly Around World After Mating, Tags Reveal," National Geographic News Web Site. Available online. URL: http://news.nationalgeographic.com/news/2005/01/0113_050113_albatross.html

———. "Birds Can See Magnetic Field." National Geographic News Web Site. Available online. URL: http://news.nationalgeographic.com/news/2007/09/070927-magnetic-birds.html

———. Great White Breaks Distance, Speed Records for Sharks." National Geographic News Web Site. Available online. URL: http://news.nationalgeographic.com/news/2005/10/1006_051006_shark_fastest.html

Schnetzer, Astrid. "Bermuda's coral reefs," Bermuda Biological Station for Research and the College of Exploration Web Site. Available online. URL: http://www.coexploration.org/bbsr/coral/html/body_astrid_schnetzer.html

Scholz, A.T., R.M. Horrall, J.C. Cooper, and A.D. Hasler. "Imprinting to Chemical Cues: The Basis for Home Stream Selection in Salmon." *Science* 192 (1976): 1247-1249.

Scott, Jonathan. "The Great Migration: The Circle of Life," Travel Africa Magazine Online Winter 1997. Available online. URL: http://www.travelafricamag.com/content/view/194/56/

Shaffer, Scott A., Yann Tremblay, Henri Weimerskirch, Darren Scott, David R. Thompson, Paul M. Sagar, Henrik Moller, Graeme A. Taylor, David G. Foley, Barbara A. Block, and Daniel P. Costa. "Migratory Shearwaters Integrate Oceanic Resources Across the Pacific Ocean in an Endless Summer." *Proceedings of the National Academy of Sciences* 103 (August 2006): 12799–12802.

Simpson, S.J., E. Despland, B.F. Hägele, and T. Dodgson. "Gregarious behavior in desert locusts is evoked by touching their back legs." *Proceedings of the National Academy of Sciences* 98 (March 2001): 3895–3897.

Slobig, Zachary. "Gray Whales Getting Thin With Warming." Discovery Channel News Web Site. Available online. URL: http://dsc.discovery.com/news/2007/07/12/thinwhales_ani_02.html?category=earth&guid=20070712090000

Tidemann, Christopher R. and John E. Nelson. "Long-distance movements of the grey-headed flying fox (Pteropus poliocephalus)." *Journal of Zoology* 263 (2004): 141–146.

United States Fish and Wildlife Service. "Clear the Way for Birds! IMBD Explores Bird Collisions," United States Fish and Wildlife Service Web Site. Available online. URL: www.fws.gov/birds/documents/Collisions.pdf

———. "Pacific Salmon, (*Oncorhynchus* spp.) Species Account," USFWS Web Site. Available online. URL: http://www.fws.gov/species/species_accounts/bio_salm.html

Waterman, Talbot Howe. *Animal Navigation*. New York: W.H. Freeman, 1989.

Wilcove, David S. *No Way Home: The Decline of the World's Great Animal Migrations*. Washington: Island Press/Shearwater Books, 2008.

Williamson, J. Michael. "WhaleNet Satellite Tagging Data, Maps, and Information," Wheelock College WhaleNet. Available online. URL: http://whale.wheelock.edu/whalenet-stuff/sat_tags_work.html

Further Resources

Cerullo, Mary M. *Sea Turtles: Ocean Nomads.* New York: Dutton's Children's Books, 2003.

Durand, Stephane and Guillaume Poyet. *Winged Migration: The Junior Edition.* San Francisco: Seuil Chronicle, 2004.

Hoyt, E. *Meeting the Whales: The Equinox Guide to Giants of the Deep.* Richmond Hill, Ontario: Firefly Books, 2000.

Knight, Tim. *Journey into Africa: A Nature Discovery Trip.* New York: Oxford University Press, 2002.

Labella, Susan. *How Animals Migrate (On the Move: Animal Migration).* Pleasantville, N.Y.: Weekly Reader, 2007.

Lerner, Carol. *On the Wing: American birds in migration.* New York: HarperCollins Publishers, 2001.

Simon, Seymour. *They Walk the Earth: The Extraordinary Travels of Animals on Land.* San Diego: Browndeer Press, 2000.

Webb, Sophie. *Looking for Seabirds: Journal from an Alaskan Voyage.* Boston: Houghton Mifflin, 2004.

Willis, Nancy Carol. *Red Knot: A shorebird's incredible journey.* Middletown, Del: Birdsong Books, 2006.

WEB SITES

BBC Radio 4 Science's "Soundscape: The Serengeti March."

http://www.bbc.co.uk/radio4/science/soundscape_serengeti.shtml

Listen to the story of a wildbeest's migration with her calf from the Serengeti Plains of East Africa to the Masai Mara and back.

Caribbean Conservation Corporation and Sea Turtle Survival League

http://cccturtle.org/ccctmp.htm

Follow migration movements of several satellite-tracked sea turtles and learn ways to help protect the species, or even adopt a turtle.

Jean-Michel Cousteau Ocean Adventures' "The Grey Whale Obstacle Course"

http://www.pbs.org/kqed/oceanadventures/episodes/whales/

Read about the gray whale's migration as chronicled in a PBS program and find out future air times

Journey North: A Global Study of Wildlife Migration and Seasonal Change

http://www.learner.org/jnorth/

Track seasonal changes through different migration patterns—such as those of monarchs, hummingbirds, and bald eagles—among other natural events.

Kansas Biological Survey, University of Kansas's "Monarch Watch"

http://www.MonarchWatch.org/

See photos, read facts, and find out ways to help—or even raise—monarchs. You also can learn about monarch migration in your area.

Operation Migration: Crane Migration

http://operationmigration.org/index.html

Learn more about Operation Migration, which taught captive reared whooping cranes a migration route after they were freed.

Smithsonian National Zoological Park's "Migratory Bird Center"

http://nationalzoo.si.edu/ConservationAndScience/MigratoryBirds/default.cfm

Learn how to help migratory birds, and try out a recipe for hummingbird nectar.

Tagging of Pacific Predators

http://www.topp.org/

Follow satellite-tagged species of top marine predators. Add a widget to your own blog so you can follow them whenever you like.

USGS Northern Prairie Wildlife Research Center's "Migration of Birds"

http://www.npwrc.usgs.gov/resource/birds/migratio/index.htm

Read the updated version of the 1935 Frederick C. Lincoln book, *Migration of Birds.*

Utah Education Network's "Shadow a Swan Project"

http://www.uen.org/swan/

Find out how your class can "shadow a swan."

Wake Forest University's "The Albatross Project"

http://www.wfu.edu/biology/albatross/index.htm

Discover different albatrosses and read about kids' studies with scientists in tracking ocean-going albatrosses.

Picture Credits

PAGE

8: © Infobase Publishing
10: Jeffrey M. Horler/Shutterstock
11: Boris Z./Shutterstock
13: Halldor Eiriksson/Shutterstock
15: NOAA/Photo Researchers, Inc.
16: Newscom
21: © Joe Austin Photography/Alamy
23: © Infobase Publishing
25: Shutterstock
27: © Infobase Publishing
31: © Brandon Cole Marine Photography/Alamy
33: David Littschwager/Getty Images
35: Ryhor M. Zasinets/Shutterstock
38: © Peter Arnold, Inc./Alamy
41: Mark R. Higgins/Shutterstock
42: Sandy Buckley/Shutterstock
45: Alan Ward/Shutterstock
48: Vera Bogaerts/Shutterstock
51: Newscom
53: Ttphoto/Shutterstock
57: © Peter Arnold, Inc./Alamy
58: Geoffrey Kuchera/Shutterstock
61: © Infobase Publishing
64: Oksana Perkins/Shutterstock
68: Lawrence Cruciana/Shutterstock
69: AFP/Getty Images
72: Stephanie Reynaud/Shutterstock
75: © blickwinkel/Alamy
77: © FLPA/Alamy
78: Eric Isselée/Shutterstock
80: © Edward Parker/Alamy
82: © Infobase Publishing
83: © Mira/Alamy
85: Shutterstock
91: © John T. Fowler/Alamy
93: Brian Dunne/Shutterstock
95: iofoto/Shutterstock
96: Lori Howard/Shutterstock
98: Frontpage/Shutterstock
99: Marie C. Fields/Shutterstock
105: Bob Blanchard/Shutterstock

Index

About the Authors

Journalist **Gretel H. Schueller** writes about science and the environment. Her articles have appeared in many magazines, such as *Audubon*, *Discover*, *National Wildlife*, *New Scientist*, *Popular Science*, and *SKI*. She was an editor at several national publications, including a kid's science magazine. Schueller is also an associate professor at the State University of New York in Plattsburgh, where she teaches journalism. She earned her master's degree in science journalism from New York University. Schueller once traveled to the tiny island of Midway, where the chatter of nearly two million Laysan albatross filled the air. Many of the birds had recently returned after a long journey at sea. She has also seen caribou herds migrating across the Alaskan tundra.

Sheila K. Schueller, Ph.D., is a senior associate at the Ecosystem Management Initiative and an adjunct consultant for the Center for Research on Learning and Teaching at the University of Michigan. She has a B.A. in Biology from Swarthmore College and a Ph.D. in Ecology and Evolutionary Biology from the University of Michigan. Her publications range from research articles on the evolution of hummingbird-pollinated plants on the California Channel Islands to practical guidebooks for natural resource managers. Schueller has been interested in animal behavior since a visit to Cape May, one of the best places to view bird migrations on the East Coast. She also has been fortunate enough to witness the Serengeti wildebeest migration in Kenya.